# THE MODERN ADVISOR PLAYBOOK

*Building a Financial Practice That Lasts*

**By Roger Kiger, CFP®**

ISBN 979-8-952030-41-1 (softcover)
ISBN 979-8-952030-42-8 (ebook)



Printed in the United States of America.

# Contents


Acknowledgement ........ v

Chapter 1: What does a Financial Advisor Actually Do? ........ 1

Chapter 2: Where to Start…and Why ........ 6

Chapter 3: Benefits to Working for a Big Firm ........ 23

Chapter 4: Benefits to Owning Your Own Practice ........ 28

Chapter 5: How do you pay for it? ........ 31

Chapter 6: What Type of Advisor Do You Want to Be When You Grow Up? ........ 38

Chapter 7: Sales – the most important thing! Is it really? ........ 44

Chapter 8: Servicing – The Key to Retention and Referrals ........ 56

Chapter 9: Using AI as the Independent Advisor's Leverage ........ 66

Chapter 10: Using AI Without Losing Your License ........ 78

Chapter 11: The Relationship Aspect ........ 83

Chapter 12: How Much is it Worth? ........ 87

Chapter 13: Can You Do It? Maybe… ........ 93

Chapter 14: Here's what I think ........ 98

Appendix ........ 101

# Acknowledgement

To my wife, Jan—

For almost 30 years, you've been my greatest supporter, my sounding board, and the patient audience for more business challenges and financial planning stories than any one person should have to endure. Thank you for standing by me through the uncertainties, late nights, endless business discussions, and the rollercoaster of starting our own business (and now, writing a book about it). Your love, laughter, and eyerolls kept me grounded—and occasionally humbled. I couldn't have done this without you, and I wouldn't have wanted to.

Content contributors:

Mac Bartine and HumanAI were helpful in providing research specifically for the chapters involving AI and compliance. Their contributions are much appreciated.

# CHAPTER 1

# What does a Financial Advisor Actually Do?

The concepts in this workbook explore the common barriers that prevent financial advisors from getting into the business or starting their own practice. It covers fears, misconceptions, and industry norms that make independence seem harder than it is. Readers will gain insight into why so many advisors stay with big firms and what it really takes to break free.

Why can't advisors work for themselves? Why should they? The industry makes too much money when advisors do NOT work for themselves or own their own practice.

Let's start by defining what a financial advisor actually does. And it is strictly my opinion, but I've been in this industry for about 30 years. I've learned a lot from smart people and have seen things I like and things I dislike. But I still believe we work in the best profession in the world and would do it all over again.

There are many misperceptions about the things we do on a daily basis. Many people think we come into the office in our Italian sports cars at 9:30 when the market opens, place a few trades on our stock screens, and then go to lunch at the country club. And the afternoon is the same way as we wrap up at 4:00 to go play 18 holes of golf. I wish this was true! These perceptions are really dated or come from movies that glamorize stockbrokers, when in fact, we don't do much of this at all.

I would break down my daily responsibility into three categories: client meetings, administrative, and analysis.

The priority that drives everything on my calendar is my client meetings. Yes, I'll meet with a wholesaler periodically or perhaps a new prospect occasionally, but the meetings with my clients are always my top priority. I'm accountable to them for the relationship and frankly, it's how we get paid. And we don't really have much choice but to work these appointments around our client's availability. We must meet when and where they have time. This won't take much time as advisors begin in the profession, but it will take up more time as the book grows. And over time, there will be less prospect meetings and more client meetings, if you are growing your practice. This probably represents 20-30% of my time.

The bulk of my time, in between appointments, is spent working on follow up items for clients, which is purely administrative. This is the task that never ends but it's also the engine that keeps things moving. And realistically, it's a large part of the value proposition we provide for clients.

For example, as part of our client review meetings, there are always follow up items such as scheduling follow up meetings, managing emails, account servicing, money transfers, or some type of research we need to do for clients. It's tedious and time consuming but these details matter and are usually the primary things for how we are judged by our clients. They want to know if we actually did the things we said we were going to do. And when I follow up to tell them I had done these tedious things, I always receive appreciation for dealing with tasks my clients don't know how to do or simply don't want to do.

The additional administrative tasks relate primarily to managing my calendar, emails, and follow up items for compliance and running my practice. The difficulty is how to organize these tasks to be sure a detail isn't missed. I rely heavily on technology for accountability as it's difficult to schedule time for these tasks. And if you miss a task or make a mistake, it can be costly in terms of damaging a client relationship or even cause financial harm to a client.

It's all glamorous, right? Not really, but it's the most important and time-consuming part of our profession, that no one ever sees. I would estimate this takes up 60% of my time. If I'm inefficient and don't know how to manage some of the tasks because it requires some research, it takes even longer. But advisors, as fiduciaries, must put the client's interest ahead of our own. This requires actual work to be sure we are completing all the details required to do just that.

And the final thing I spend time working on is research. But it's not research in looking at stock screens or trading futures and options. I spend time looking at analytics in clients' accounts. I'm generally looking to see if their overall allocation is within its risk tolerance or checking the performance to be sure we're on track with their goals. On a monthly or quarterly basis, I do spend time evaluating positions and allocations based on the current market cycles, but this can get time consuming and be a real distraction from the follow up administrative tasks that are crucial. Overall, I would estimate that I spend 10-20% of my time on these things.

As you can see, how we actually spend our time each day is much different from how clients think we spend our time. And the priorities change drastically as our practice grows and evolves from a sales driven practice to a service driven firm.

The financial industry is enormous and very fragmented. It includes many types of products, services, corporate structures, and sizes, and can be divided into multiple silos. For the purposes of our discussions, we'll be discussing primarily the investment management realm, and it'll be limited strictly to advisors who work directly with retail clients. This is further narrowed down to the Registered Investment Advisor practice and may include broker dealer channels, although the BD business should not be considered the primary business channel.

As a matter of opinion, and I feel strongly about this, the fiduciary standard is the only way to practice for financial advisors. Fee based asset management and financial planning has emerged as the leading financial advisor model over the past 15 years and will continue to grow exponentially as advisors and clients continue to move assets away from commission-based products and services and move them to fee-based assets. And I believe it's better for clients!

However, I will never agree that all clients should be in fee-only accounts alone. In fact, there are many reasons for clients to have commission-based products and services, but they are very specific and in some cases are the only investment vehicles available. Therefore, it doesn't make sense to paint the industry with a broad brush and assume everyone should work with a fee-only advisory firm.

In fact, I would go a step further and say that advisors who adopt the "fee only" model, are not honoring their fiduciary duty for clients. It's hard to understand how any advisor can make the statement they are a "fiduciary" for their clients, but aren't willing to service some types of investments, or even consider them for a clients' specific needs. Therefore, I believe the fee-based model is much better than the fee-only model.

There is one final misperception that warrants some attention. Most people think our jobs are easy. In my opinion, if your financial advising job is easy, you are doing it wrong. There are so many things an independent advisor must manage effectively, and they all take immense amounts of time to handle correctly. Let's separate these tasks into client-oriented tasks and operational tasks.

The client-oriented tasks seem straight forward. This depends on your practice, but with the onset of AI as a competitor, the client-oriented tasks just got easier if you are utilizing the AI tools available. And it will force you to be more comprehensive for your clients. There is more technology available for financial planning, CRM, investment allocations, and especially for business development. If you aren't using AI tools to scale these tasks, you will fall behind the firms that do. I know this seems like a lot to manage, but frankly, this only addresses the client tasks, and this will likely consume your first 30-40 hours per week.

The main tasks that are overlooked are the operational tasks. How hard can they be, right? If this is your opinion, you need to do some research. While AI is a great tool to help advisors, it's also a great tool to help cyber thieves. Cybersecurity, infrastructure, E&O insurance, compliance and technology tools for operations are also things that need ongoing attention. If they don't get your attention from a preventive perspective, they'll certainly get your attention once an issue arises, and it will happen, so once again, you must use the tools available to scale your time. And this will likely take another 10-20 hours per week if done efficiently.

If this sounds like too much work, you are correct. You must be an entrepreneur and really want your own practice to be able to wear all these hats simultaneously. You must be able to adopt technology, manage your time, and still prioritize your client facing tasks. Most importantly, you must do the work. Otherwise, you should consider joining a firm who will allow you to own your book or remain somewhat independent. I cannot stress this enough…

As I talk through these concepts, you'll hear me repeat may euphemisms that you've heard for years in our industry. Why do I keep repeating these things? Because they are all true!

You won't hear me quote a lot of sources for statistics or authors of business writings or even great financial advisors. There are many great thought leaders. They are all helpful and you should research them all, find one or two you respect, and follow them with diligence.

My concepts come completely from my experience, some have been great, and a few…not so much. But that's how we learn, and those are the experiences I hope will provide value to others.

# CHAPTER 2

# Where to Start...and Why

How are you supposed to get started? Are desire and commitment enough? Not likely.

How hard can it be, right? The biggest issue with folks wanting to be an advisor is where to start. It's virtually impossible to get licensed and immediately go into practice for yourself. There are a so many barriers and requirements that we can't cover them all. But let's cover a few of the obstacles.

The first barrier is "Not knowing what you don't know". Let's face it, everyone thinks starting your own advisory firm is easy, right? If you can stick it out financially through the first couple of years, you should be OK. Wrong!

When I say this is wrong, I'm not being judgmental. It's exactly what I did, mainly because I didn't know any better. But I had some business experience, and I had over 10 years of industry experience. And I still made a lot of mistakes that cost time and money.

There are so many more things to consider. And the list of things to consider is based entirely on the type of practice you want to build, the type of clients you want to attract and your plan to get there. If you haven't been in the business for a few years, the barriers might become fatal mistakes. The primary challenge is building revenue before running out of reserves.

The second obstacle is experience. Many folks begin by working in an administrative position or a sales position selling insurance. But getting licensed is the easy part. Most of the entry level positions don't pay well and make it difficult to make a long-term living. And if you do work for another firm to gain experience, they will likely tie up your client base with non-solicitations and non-compete agreements. And while these may not be career ending, they are real barriers to exiting those firms to start your own practice.

But everyone must start somewhere. And when you decide to be your own advisor, you won't have the luxury of time to learn the business. So, wherever you land as an entry into the profession, take the time and learn everything you can. While you might not get paid much, I would argue that part of your compensation is the experience you gain, regardless of where you are working in the financial industry.

I began my career working for a national firm who accepted almost anyone into their "training" program. Sure, I passed the aptitude and compatibility test with a score of 95%. But after just one year, it became apparent to me the plan was for me to sell insurance to all my family and friends.

Throughout my first year, I generated about $60,000 in commissions, which was OK by the firms' standards. After I paid for leads, rented their office, and paid their fees, I came home with about $11,000. And I was working in my family restaurant at night to pay the bills. As it turns out, I was not a good salesperson.

But I did gain some valuable experience. I learned to use financial planning as my basis for every recommendation. And I learned that every client I met with, had some type of financial need, that I always uncovered with a financial plan. This determined my path as a financial planner, as I really enjoyed the "big picture" aspect of dealing with client's financial future.

After 11 months, the firm had hired 19 advisors and only 9 were left. And when a group of us worked together, we were hired by a bank to start a financial planning division. Thus began my next 11 years in banking as a financial planner.

The tangible and intangible compensation you gain during your early years, perhaps working with a larger firm, includes a few really important things:

**1) How to Deal with People – Selling Yourself is Key**

Success as a financial advisor is not just about understanding investments—it's about understanding people. Clients don't just buy financial plans; they buy trust, confidence, and relationships. This means being a great communicator, listening to client concerns, and presenting yourself as the expert they need. Advisors must master personal branding, networking, and building long-term client relationships to establish credibility and grow their business.

Financial advising is a relationship-driven business. No matter how knowledgeable an advisor is, success hinges on the ability to connect with clients, build trust, and demonstrate value.

- Personal Branding: Clients need to feel confident that they're working with a professional they can trust. Young advisors should develop a clear, authentic personal brand that communicates expertise, reliability, and integrity.
- Active Listening & Communication: Great advisors listen more than they speak. Understanding a client's needs, fears, and goals is crucial to providing tailored advice.
- Storytelling & Persuasion: Numbers and data don't sell—stories do. The best advisors use relatable examples and real-life scenarios to help clients understand complex financial concepts.
- Networking & Referrals: Building a book of business is an ongoing process. Advisors should invest in networking, attending industry events, and asking satisfied clients for referrals.
- Confidence & Presence: Clients need to feel that their advisor is confident in their recommendations. This means speaking with certainty, dressing professionally, and presenting ideas with clarity.

New advisors should focus on relationship-building as much as technical skills. Without the ability to sell themselves, even the best financial knowledge won't translate into success. And to sell yourself successfully, you must believe in yourself. We'll cover more of this later.

**2) Investment Experience – You Have to Be Able to Do More Than Pick a Good Stock**

Many young advisors enter the field thinking their job is to find the best stocks or investment strategies. While investment knowledge is important, the real value advisors provide is in financial planning, risk management, and helping clients navigate life events. A good advisor understands asset allocation, tax implications, estate planning, and behavioral finance. The focus should be on guiding clients to make informed decisions rather than simply trying to outperform the market.

Many young advisors assume their job is to find the best investments for clients. While investment selection is important, financial advising is about holistic financial planning rather than just investment analysis.

- Financial Planning First: Advisors must help clients with retirement planning, tax strategies, estate planning, insurance needs, and cash flow management. Investments are just one piece of the puzzle.
- Risk Management: A great advisor understands how to assess a client's risk tolerance and structure a portfolio accordingly. The ability to balance risk and return is more valuable than finding the next hot stock.
- Behavioral Finance: Clients often make emotional investment decisions. Advisors must act as financial psychologists, helping clients stay disciplined during market volatility and avoid costly mistakes. We become counselors and clients share financial secrets with us they cannot share with anyone else.
- Investment Vehicles Beyond Stocks: Bonds, ETFs, mutual funds, REITs, annuities, and alternative investments all play a role in portfolio construction. Advisors must be well-versed in multiple asset classes.
- Long-Term Thinking: The best advisors focus on helping clients achieve long-term financial goals rather than chasing short-term market trends.

- And yes, you must understand investment allocations. And while this seems simple on the surface and many advisors think they can do it because they've watched too many movies, it's a lot of work to do this correctly.

The most successful financial advisors act as trusted guides rather than investment pickers. Their value lies in strategic planning and financial coaching, not just selecting individual stocks.

**3) Learning how to Fail in This Profession – If You Are Going to Make Mistakes, Do It with Oversight**

Mistakes are inevitable in any career, but in financial advising, they can have real consequences for clients and an advisor's reputation. New advisors should seek mentorship, work under experienced professionals, and follow structured processes to minimize risks. Being transparent about errors, learning from them, and continuously improving is key. This chapter would emphasize that failure is part of growth and that those who learn from their early missteps are the ones who succeed long-term.

Failure is a reality in financial advising, but the key is failing the right way—with safeguards in place to protect clients and minimize damage.

- Common Mistakes New Advisors Make:
    - Overpromising returns to clients
    - Focusing too much on sales and not enough on service
    - Not asking enough questions to fully understand a client's needs
    - Avoiding difficult conversations (e.g., discussing risk or budgeting)
    - Letting emotions dictate investment decisions
    - Picking one investment allocation and think it's OK. This is also a common thought for clients who don't understand the depth of this process.
- The Importance of Mentorship: New advisors should work under experienced professionals who can review recommendations, provide feedback, and prevent major missteps.

- Compliance & Regulations: Advisors must follow strict industry regulations to avoid legal trouble. Working within a structured compliance framework can prevent costly errors.
- Owning Mistakes & Learning Quickly: Every advisor will give bad advice at some point. The key is owning the mistake, fixing it, and learning from it rather than letting it derail a career. And it's OK to tell a client, "I don't know, but I'll figure it out".
- Developing a Resilient Mindset: Advisors must handle rejection, difficult clients, and market downturns. Building resilience and learning from failure is essential for long-term success.
- This part of an advisor's journey should encourage young advisors to fail fast, fail small, and fail under supervision—so that their mistakes become steppingstones rather than career-ending events. If you learn from your mistakes, don't repeat them, and teach someone else about them, the mistakes translate into experience.

**4) Guaranteed Income While You Learn the Industry**

One of the biggest hurdles for new advisors is financial stability while they build their practice. Unlike traditional jobs, many advisory roles have commission-based structures, meaning income is unpredictable at first. This section would explore options like working under a salary-based role at a firm, hybrid compensation models, or taking on a side income source while developing a client base. The goal is to provide a financial cushion that allows new advisors to focus on growth without the stress of immediate financial pressure.

One of the biggest challenges a new advisor faces is income uncertainty. Many firms operate on the "Eat what you kill" model, meaning advisors may not make much money in their first year. Having some financial stability while ramping up is critical.

- Salary-Based Roles: Some large firms offer salary-based positions for new advisors. These roles provide financial security while allowing advisors to build experience before transitioning to a commission model.

- Hybrid Compensation Models: Some firms offer a base salary plus commission structure, giving new advisors a safety net while they grow their book of business.
- Financial Planning Support Roles: Working as a paraplanner, analyst, or associate advisor can provide steady income while learning the industry. These positions allow young professionals to gain hands-on experience without the pressure of immediate sales.
- Side Hustles & Supplemental Income: Many new advisors take on part-time jobs, freelance work, or financial education roles to supplement their income while building their client base. Teaching financial literacy courses, writing blogs, or consulting on budgeting are good ways to earn money while staying in the industry.
- Firm-Sponsored Programs: Some firms offer training stipends or forgivable loans to help new advisors get started. It's worth researching which firms provide the best financial support during the early years. This is the model our firm has adopted as we try to give advisors and entry into the profession, assuming they have some experience.

Young advisors should plan on not having income as an independent advisor for the first 12–24 months as a financial runway—having guaranteed income in the early stages can mean the difference between quitting and building a successful practice.

In summary, each of these topics highlights critical lessons that every young financial advisor must learn to thrive in the industry.

- Selling yourself and building relationships is just as important as technical knowledge.
- Investment selection is a small part of a bigger financial planning picture.
- Mistakes are inevitable, learning from them is what matters.
- Income stability early on can make or break a young advisor's career.

After you have a few years' experience and you get your investment licenses, you'll have more options. And you'll likely start to narrow down your desired path in the financial industry. Whether you want to manage client relationships or portfolios, a few years' experience, will give you an idea of what position you enjoy the most, and narrow down your path.

Here's where it starts to get tricky. As many advisors start to advance through different levels of financial firms, the income begins to get better, and the quality of life begins to greatly improve. This is where most folks find a lane with their current firm and stay in it. As we get more secure, learn to appreciate the firm that helped us get started, and mature into adult life stages, it gets more and more difficult to leave the security of a longer career to start over as an investment advisor with little or no job security after a potential transition.

Short-Term Thinking Can Trap You in Long-Term Situations

Many aspiring financial advisors make career decisions based on short-term concerns like immediate cash flow, job security, and benefits. While these are valid considerations, they can lead to long-term career limitations if they dictate major choices.

The Short-Term Trap

New advisors often feel pressure to:

- Take a safe salary-based job instead of building their own practice.
- Stay at a firm that doesn't align with their long-term goals because of initial stability.
- Prioritize short-term earnings over gaining valuable experience.

While these decisions might provide temporary relief, they can create long-term dissatisfaction by locking advisors into roles that don't fit their true ambitions.

Why Short-Term Issues Resolve Over Time

- Cash Flow Improves: While income may be inconsistent at first, successful advisors build a client base that eventually leads to stable, recurring revenue.

- Job Security Comes with Performance: Unlike traditional jobs, financial advising offers unlimited earning potential for those who grow their practice. Security comes from building strong client relationships, not from a salary.
- Benefits Can Be Replaced: While working independently may mean giving up employer-provided benefits initially, advisors who succeed earn enough to afford better personal benefits packages.

Passion Drives Success (and Income Follows)! I know this to be true because I proved it. I didn't have a manual or a blueprint. I knew how to start a business from experience, and I knew how I wanted to take care of my clients. I had seen the mistakes made by the firms I had worked for previously. And at that point, necessity became the mother of invention, and failure was not an option.

If you love what you do, you will naturally:

- Work harder and smarter.
- Provide better service to clients.
- Stay committed during challenging times.
- And you'll never "work" a day in life of your career.

Advisors who choose a path they are passionate about tend to make more money in the long run, because their enthusiasm translates into better results, stronger client relationships, and ultimately higher earnings.

The Danger of Letting Short-Term Issues Dictate Long-Term Decisions

One of the biggest mistakes young financial advisors make is basing their long-term career choices on short-term financial concerns. It's easy to get stuck in a job or career path that isn't fulfilling just because it feels financially safe at the time. But security today doesn't always mean success or satisfaction in the future. If it's part of a larger plan, it can work.

While these concerns are real, they shouldn't be the sole deciding factors in shaping your career—because they often resolve over time with success. But when your position is eliminated unexpectedly while working for someone else, you plan is changed for you, and you don't get an opinion.

After I had worked in the profession for about a year and gained some sales experience, I was offered a job at a bank. I thought this would be where I would stay for my career. It had a salary, benefits, a great work environment and most of all, career stability. But my perspective was entirely wrong. After just two years, the bank was bought by a bigger bank, which led to a series of mergers and buyouts. This resulted in my position having a new boss every year or two. And when a new boss or bank takes over, there is no consideration given to tenure, performance, or quality of life. It's a new deal, and you must perform. And perform is exactly what I did. Because of my business experience, I understood the deal, even though it always changed. But after 10+ years of it, I became exhausted with the routine, the poor client service, and the endless transitions.

The Long-Term Cost of Short-Term Thinking

Making career decisions based solely on immediate financial security can lead to long-term stagnation, such as:

- Being stuck in a firm that doesn't align with your values – If you take a job just for the paycheck, you might find yourself following policies and sales tactics you don't believe in.
- Missing out on the freedom to build your own brand – Many large firms have strict rules on client interactions, marketing, and investment strategies, limiting your personal and professional growth.
- Capping your income potential – Salary-based roles offer stability but often come with earning limits, while building your own practice provides uncapped growth potential over time.

Why These Short-Term Issues Solve Themselves

While cash flow, security, and benefits seem like immediate obstacles, successful advisors naturally overcome them as they progress in their careers:

- Cash Flow Improves – With time, advisors build a book of business that provides a steady stream of income through fees and recurring revenue.
- Job Security Comes from Performance – Unlike traditional jobs, financial advising rewards those who take control of their careers. Once an advisor has built strong client relationships, their security is based on their skills, not an employer.
- Benefits Become a Non-Issue – Successful independent advisors eventually earn enough to purchase their own health insurance, retirement plans, and even better perks than they would receive from an employer.

As you can see, it's easy to take the "safe" path early on, but advisors should ask themselves:

- Am I choosing this role because it aligns with my future goals, or just because it feels financially comfortable today?
- Will this position allow me to grow into the kind of advisor I want to be?
- Am I making decisions out of fear, or based on where I truly want to go?

While it's important to manage short-term financial needs, they should never dictate long-term career choices. The best advisors play the long game, stay patient, and trust that their hard work will pay off in the end. Spend more time making longer term decisions and use a long-term perspective.

**The Bottom Line**

Short-term struggles shouldn't dictate long-term career choices. Advisors should focus on where they ultimately want to be and trust that financial success will follow with time, effort, and persistence.

I would argue that it's easy to get stuck in long term scenarios based on short term issues. And short-term issues are mostly cash flow, job security, and benefits. But these things will come with time and success as an advisor, even if working for a larger firm. If you are doing what you like, you'll do a better job, and the money will come eventually.

The next issue is folks are afraid to trust themselves as advisors. It's a lot of responsibility when your first client asks you how to invest their life savings, and you realize the level of fiduciary duty you have. Now we're back to that experience we mentioned earlier. Follow your training, job experience, and the resources around you before you jeopardize someone's life savings. This is why most firms don't let new advisors make recommendations or invest funds by themselves. They normally must involve a mentor or supervisor. And we're back to that experience issue we've mentioned several times…

Here are a few more challenges that continually evolve as our industry continues to grow, fragments, and requires more oversight. And I'll make the statement that it's becoming more difficult to be independent due to increasing costs for technology, compliance, etc.

First challenge: Financial Advisors Are Not Business-Minded People—But They Think They Are.

Many financial advisors believe they have a strong business mindset simply because they work with money and investments. However, understanding financial markets and managing client portfolios is not the same as running a successful business. The reality is that many advisors struggle with the entrepreneurial aspects of their career, and those who don't develop true business acumen often hit a ceiling in their success. They must learn to run the practice more like a business. And they must stop believing social media when they see all the advertisements stating that "anyone can own their own business". Becoming an independent advisor is much more complex than owning a small business.

## Why Advisors Think They're Business-Minded

Many advisors mistakenly believe that:

- Their knowledge of investments and financial planning means they understand business operations.
- Their ability to manage client money translates into the ability to manage a company's revenue, expenses, and profitability.
- Selling financial services is the same as marketing and growing a sustainable business.
- Because they are independent or commission-based, they are already an "entrepreneur" without having true business systems in place.

## The Key Differences Between Advisors and Business Owners

A great financial advisor may excel at helping clients reach their financial goals, but running a business requires a completely different skill set. Business-minded individuals focus on:

1. Building Systems, Not Just Clients
    - Advisors often think more clients = success, but real business owners understand that systems create sustainable, scalable success.
    - Without efficient operations, client service models, and automation, advisors will be stuck in an endless cycle of chasing new business instead of running a thriving practice.
2. Marketing & Branding (Not Just Networking)
    - Many advisors rely on word-of-mouth and referrals, assuming that's all they need.
    - True business owners invest in marketing, digital presence, brand building, and lead generation to create predictable growth.
3. Profitability, Sales, & Financial Management (Beyond Commissions & Fees)
    - Advisors focus on growing assets under management (AUM), but business owners focus on profitability, efficiency, and reinvesting for growth.

- A real business mindset includes tracking expenses, optimizing revenue streams, and maximizing margins, not just increasing client assets.

4. Scaling & Hiring for Growth
   - Advisors often operate as solo practitioners, thinking that hiring staff will cut into their income.
   - Business owners understand that delegating non-client-facing tasks (admin work, marketing, compliance) allows them to scale their practice and increase overall revenue.
5. Exit Strategy & Long-Term Value
   - Many advisors work year to year without thinking about what they are building.
   - A true business owner asks: What is my practice worth? Can I sell it one day? Am I creating long-term enterprise value?

How Advisors Can Develop a True Business Mindset

To transition from a financial advisor to a true business owner, advisors must shift their perspective. Instead of just thinking about their next client meeting, they need to think about their business as a whole.

- Create a business plan – What are your revenue goals? How will you scale?
- Invest in marketing – Don't just rely on referrals. Build a brand.
- Optimize processes – Automate tasks and use technology to improve efficiency.
- Think beyond your own work hours – A real business makes money even when you're not working.
- Realize that building a business is a team sport. The people you surround yourself with really matter.
- Plan an exit strategy – Your business should be an asset you can sell or pass on.

Most financial advisors are not truly business-minded—but they can become business-minded with the right mindset shift. The key is realizing that running a practice is not just about managing clients' money—it's about running a profitable, scalable, and valuable business.

Second Challenge: Don't know how to think out of the box-always been told they can't do it!

How to Start Thinking Outside the Box

◇ Challenge the Industry Norms

Instead of accepting things at face value, ask:

- Why is this the "normal" way? Is there a better way?
- What are other industries doing that we could adapt to financial advising?
- What frustrates me about this business, and how can I fix it?

◇ Reinvent the Client Experience

Most advisors follow the same sales approach and client interaction process. Instead of blending in, consider:

- Could I offer a subscription-based advisory service instead of traditional AUM fees?
- Can I provide financial planning for a niche market that others ignore?
- Can I make financial advising more engaging through content, social media, or interactive tools?

◇ Leverage Technology in New Ways

- Many advisors still rely on old-school cold calling and referrals. Why not try:
  - Hosting live webinars or Q&A sessions on financial topics?
  - Using automated marketing funnels to attract and nurture clients?
  - Creating a financial podcast or YouTube channel to build credibility?

◇ Surround Yourself with Forward Thinkers, COI, Advisory boards

- If you only talk to other traditional advisors, you'll think like them.
- Engage with entrepreneurs, tech innovators, and marketing experts to gain fresh perspectives.

- Join mastermind groups, attend non-financial industry conferences, and read business books that challenge conventional thinking.

◇ Give Yourself Permission to Experiment!

- You won't break the industry by trying something different.
- Test small changes in your practice—see what works and adapt.
- The most successful advisors aren't the ones who followed the rules perfectly—they're the ones who figured out a better way.

---

Final Thoughts

Advisors who never think outside the box stay stuck in the same patterns—relying on outdated methods, struggling to stand out, and limiting their income potential.

The best advisors ask, "What if?"

- What if I structured my practice differently?
- What if I reached clients in a new way?
- What if I stopped worrying about what I was told I couldn't do and focused on what I could?

Breaking free from a limiting mindset isn't easy, but it's the difference between being an average advisor and becoming a leader in the industry.

Third Challenge: Assuming the way you've always done is the way you should always do it.

Perhaps it's safe to stay consistent with your client service model. Clients like consistency in everything you do for them. It gives them comfort and security to be familiar with our habits, our technology, and even our office location.

But the operations of our practice must continually change. The technology is always changing, and we must continue to adapt with it. This includes compliance, operations, trading, and how we maintain client data. This change is inevitable as tech firms are bought and sold through M&A. And compliance rules will change regarding how we handle certain tasks for clients. Even the custodians will update the processes for trading or sending out client statements. These are industry changes we must be accustomed to managing with minimal impact to our clients.

Our firm uses over 9 technology platforms alone. But we are a little different. As an independent firm, we've chosen each one for a specific task to customize our business model. And each platform will undergo updates and changes independently. Some larger firms don't have that option as they adopt technology across the company, and everyone will be forced to use it.

We haven't yet touched on how AI can help or hurt our practice. It's not something we can disregard as just another passing fad or trend. It's a real game changer and will likely change our profession over the next 5-10 years. Most of the change will be a great thing, but many advisors will struggle with the change. Again, we cannot fight technology, we can only adapt and change with it. More to come on this later.

While we might be struggling the challenges of change, we cannot pass these struggles along to our clients as this type of change makes them uneasy. But it's part of the job and it's what we are paid to do. And the hope is that these changes make our practice more efficient or provide additional benefits to our clients. Therefore, we must adapt along the way.

## CHAPTER 3

# Benefits to Working for a Big Firm

While independence offers flexibility, creativity, and ownership, working for a large firm provides stability, structure, training, and valuable resources. For many advisors, starting their careers in a wire house, bank, or large financial institution is a strategic decision that provides essential experience, mentorship, and security before deciding whether to go independent.

This chapter explores the advantages of working for a big firm and how advisors can use this experience to build a strong foundation for long-term success.

Begin at a Wire house or bank? Maybe. There Are Real Benefits.

I know we've mentioned this before, but there's a reason why many of the most successful financial advisors begin their careers at a major financial institution. And some advisors never leave. These firms provide an environment that allows new advisors to learn, grow professionally, and establish credibility in the industry.

1. Gain real world experience.

One of the most understated benefits of working at a big firm is learning from their seasoned advisors. Observing their successes, and their failures, and learning invaluable insights that can help shape your approach.

Textbooks and financial certifications can only teach you so much. Working in a structured environment gives you hands on experience in client interactions, portfolio management, and navigating industry challenges such as market cycles, compliance, and industry changes.

It's difficult to put a value on this level of experience. If you are trying to do this on your own, while trying to build a practice, you'll need to add all this training into your daily schedule. And assuming you find a mentor or organization that lets you do it free of charge, it's still a huge opportunity cost because it's time when you aren't earning income. And this is a period of years, not weeks or months of training.

2. Infrastructure-They have a plan

Banks and wire houses have done this before. They are money making machines, primarily because they are publicly traded and must drive profits. Therefore, they've refined the process over the years to provide solutions to your biggest obstacles. And in their perfect world, they make more money with lifelong employees who can work within this model. More on this shortly.

My personal experience:

While I sound like I'm being hard on the institutions, I'm not. I spent the first 11 years of my career working for regional banks. I will never discount the experiences I learned there, and the connections I made. But more than anything else, it gave me the perspective I needed regarding how I wanted to spend the rest of my career. The banks were good to me. I made a great living, started a family with financial security, and built a nice nest egg. But I wanted more for my clients, which is why I eventually decided to leave the bank and start my own firm. But I'll never regret my time or experience working for the banks as I could not have gained the experience and insight without "putting in my time" with a big firm.

3. The "Country Club" Lifestyle

Large firms often come with a built-in prestige factor and instant credibility. Whether it's the reputation of a well-known wire house or the trust associated with a respected bank, being part of a big-name institution provides instant confidence. This can open doors to high-net-worth clients, networking opportunities, and social circles that would be difficult to access as an independent advisor.

### 4. Strong Employee Benefits

Unlike independent advisors who must handle their own healthcare, retirement plans, and other benefits, employees at large firms typically receive:

- Health insurance
- 401(k) matching
- Paid time off
- Bonuses and incentives
- Expense accounts

These perks can make a significant difference in the early years of an advisor's career, especially when income is unpredictable, life is changing rapidly, and financial security grows in importance.

### 5. Predictable Hours and Work-Life Balance

While financial advising is never a 9-to-5 job, working for a big firm typically comes with more structure and stability than running your own practice. Independent advisors often spend extra hours handling marketing, operations, and compliance, while large-firm advisors can focus more on client relationships and financial planning within set hours.

### 6. A Great Way to Gain Experience and Learn the Business—But Don't Take Your Clients

Starting a career in a wire house or bank is one of the best ways to learn the ins and outs of the industry. You'll gain direct experience working with clients, understanding financial products, and managing relationships. However, firms are very protective of their clients, and trying to take them with you when you leave can result in legal and financial consequences. The key is to use this experience to build skills and industry knowledge before deciding on your long-term career path. And when you sign the non-solicitation agreement or the non-compete agreement, you'll need to honor it down the road. There are ways to work through these issues if you leave and clients call you, but you should read through the agreement before you sign it and ask questions. It will come back to visit you in the future.

7. Build Your Centers of Influence (COI)

One of the most valuable aspects of working for a big firm is the opportunity to build relationships with professionals who can refer business to you. These might include:

- Attorneys
- CPAs
- Business owners
- Mortgage brokers
- Bankers

Establishing these connections early in your career can create a foundation for future growth, whether you stay with the firm or go independent later. But this takes a lot of time, effort, and introductions that come with experience. And if done correctly, will shape the future of your career regardless of where you work. More to come on this in another chapter.

8. Learn from Others' Mistakes and Experience

There are so many potential mistakes to be made. This is part of the reasons the bigger firms have credibility. They have the resources and procedures to prevent them and potentially, deal with them when they happen. Errors and mistakes are part of this profession. If you aren't prepared to work hard to prevent them, you should be prepared to own them when they happen and pay for them to resolve them. It's difficult, but it will happen.

This is where a "shared" responsibility is helpful. When you work for a large firm as a new advisor, most advisors work in teams which include a younger advisor and a seasoned advisor. This is helpful to everyone on the team, especially when you realize the level of responsibility that comes with the decisions and recommendations we must make for our clients. This cannot be emphasized enough. And it makes no sense for inexperienced advisors to try to make decisions for clients without this level of experience.

My personal experience:

One of my biggest mistakes was made soon after I started my own practice. I had a good client that owned several stocks with a very low-cost basis. We had agreed on a 4-year strategy to sell them and spread out the capital gains exposure. This worked well the first year, but during the second year, I rebalanced the account and completely forgot about our predetermined plan. I sold all the stocks and generated a huge capital gain. And once you "push the button, there's no going back.

I realized the mistake and called to tell him about it. He was really surprised this happened since we had several discussions about our plan. But he was more surprised that I owned the mistake and agreed to pay the additional tax that it might have cost him. It was the right thing to do. This was an expensive lesson and really hurt to pay for when I was young in my independent career. And it was NOT covered by my errors and omissions insurance.

Ironically, this also proved something else to the client. It proved he could trust me. And when his family unexpectedly came into a large inheritance several years later, he never talked to anyone else about managing his money. His trust in me and my firm made his decision simple. Now he's one of the larger and longest tenured clients at our firm.

But it's bigger than that. He trusts us at every level, and we're engaged with every aspect of his family's financial life. And that's the type of client I'm always looking to earn respect from.

## CHAPTER 4

# Benefits to Owning Your Own Practice

Owning a financial advisory practice is both a financial and personal growth opportunity. It comes with challenges and advantages—such as control over client relationships, unlimited income potential, a flexible work-life balance, and long-term equity- which make it an attractive path for many advisors. This chapter explores the key benefits of independence while acknowledging the realities that come with it.

Being Independent Allows Creativity

One of the biggest perks of running your own practice is the freedom to design it your way. Unlike large firms that dictate how advisors interact with clients, invest, and operate, independence allows you to shape your business to fit your strengths and preferences and personalize your service for your clients.

1. Lack of Corporate Structure Helps Attract Like-Minded Clients

At a big firm, you're often assigned clients based on the firm's priorities. As an independent advisor, you have the power to attract and work with people who share your values, financial philosophy, and approach to planning. This alignment fosters deeper trust and longer-lasting relationships. And clients tend to work with advisor who share the same views, have the same hobbies, and are in the same phase of life. After all, most of the discussions during meetings will NOT be about portfolio management. They'll be about personal experiences and life transitions.

2. Matching Communication Styles, Lifestyles, and Personal Investing Philosophies

Every client is unique. Some prefer detailed, analytical discussions, while others want a simplified, high-level overview. Some clients are risk-tolerant entrepreneurs, while others are conservative retirees. Independence allows you to communicate and work in ways that feel natural to you and your clients, making relationships smoother and more effective.

3. Customizing Your Practice Focus

No advisor excels at everything—some thrive in financial planning, others in investment strategy, tax planning, or business consulting. At a large firm, you may be pressured to provide services outside your strengths or interests. Owning your practice gives you the ability to specialize and work in the areas where you add the most value.

4. Loving What You Do, Who You Do It For, and Who You Do It With, Leads to Long-Term Success

When you enjoy your work, the people you work with, and the clients you serve, it naturally leads to better outcomes. Passion fuels motivation, and over time, this builds a strong reputation that attracts more of the right clients. The financial rewards will follow.

5. It's Not About Picking Stocks—It's About Building Relationships

Many people think financial advising is about finding the best investments, but the reality is far deeper. True advisors build strong, long-term relationships with their clients. Their worries become your worries. Their successes become your successes, and their hardships also become yours. This is what will keep you awake at night. But this level of care and commitment is what sets great advisors apart.

## The Best Part Is What You Take, Not Just What You Give

When you own your practice, you don't just serve your clients—you're invested in the entire process. Your business is yours, and that personal stake makes everything feel more meaningful. Clients will see the difference, too.

- They'll sense your commitment and reciprocate with trust and loyalty.
- They'll share insights with you that they wouldn't discuss at a big firm.
- They'll provide feedback that helps you grow, both professionally and personally.
- Over time, the lessons you learn from your clients will be just as valuable—if not more—than the lessons you teach them.

Owning a practice isn't for everyone, but for those who take the leap, the benefits are significant. You control your business, your clients, and your future. The trade-off is the responsibility and risk that comes with it, but it will drive what you do every day and challenge you in ways you never thought possible. But if you are organized, focused, and thoughtful, the challenge is worth it.

## CHAPTER 5

# How do you pay for it?

After everything we've covered in the previous chapter, there's an even bigger issue, which is how to pay for the practice when you start from scratch. Should you finance the business with time, your own money, or debt?

Starting a financial advisory practice requires time or capital, but the way you finance your business will impact your long-term success. Many new advisors face a crucial decision: Should I build my practice over time using sweat equity, or should I take on debt to accelerate growth? At this point, I'm assuming you are starting a practice without any existing clients.

While both approaches have their merits, avoiding debt is often not the best strategy. Here's why.

Option 1: Financing Your Business with Time (Sweat Equity Approach)

Building a practice over time without taking on debt means you'll rely on personal savings, early client revenue, and cost-conscious business strategies. This approach may be slower, but it allows for sustainable growth without financial pressure.

Advantages of Financing with Time:

☑ Low Risk, High Control – Without loan payments, you have the freedom to make business decisions without financial stress.

☑ Sustainable Growth – You build your client base gradually, ensuring you provide quality service rather than scrambling to cover expenses.
☑ No Pressure to Sell Just for Revenue – Advisors who take on debt often feel forced to chase commissions, leading to short-term thinking and questionable sales practices.
☑ Retains Business Equity – If you take on investors or partners for capital, you may have to give up control of your business. Financing with time keeps you in charge.

Challenges of the Time-Based Approach:

* Slower Growth – Without capital to invest in marketing or hiring, growth takes longer.
*Lower Initial Income – The early months (or years) may involve financial strain as you build a client base. And the marketing efforts take a long time to see a return on any investments.

Option 2: Financing with Money (Taking on Debt or Investors)

Some advisors choose to take out a loan, business line of credit, or seek investors to fund their practice upfront. This approach provides quick access to resources, but it also comes with risks and obligations.

Potential Advantages of Financing with Your Money:

☑ Faster Growth – Capital allows you to invest in marketing, hire staff, and acquire clients more quickly.
☑ Immediate Infrastructure – You can set up office space, technology, and branding at a professional level from day one.
☑ Higher Initial Earnings Potential – With more capital, you can start earning sooner rather than waiting for organic growth.

The Major Risks of Taking on Debt:

* Financial Stress – Loan payments create pressure, which can lead to bad business decisions.
* Reduced Flexibility – You might feel forced to take on any client

(even bad ones) just to meet financial obligations.
* No Guarantee of Success – Even with funding, an advisor still needs to build relationships and trust—money alone doesn't create clients.
*Interest Costs Cut Into Profits – Instead of reinvesting in the business, a portion of revenue goes to repaying debt.
* Potential Loss of Business Ownership – If you take on investors, you might lose control of your practice or owe a percentage of profits indefinitely.

Why Avoiding Debt is the Best Strategy

Many businesses rely on debt to grow, but financial advisors have a unique advantage: the business requires very little capital to start compared to other industries. Unlike restaurants or retail stores that need inventory, leases, and equipment, financial advisors can start lean and scale up gradually.

Instead of taking on debt, consider these alternative funding strategies:

- Start with a Low-Cost Model – Work from home or use shared office space instead of leasing an expensive office.
- Use Commission or Fee Revenue to Reinvest in Growth – Instead of borrowing money upfront, let your early client revenue fund expansion.
- Consider Part-Time Work Initially – If needed, keep a side job while you build your practice.
- Leverage Digital Marketing – Use cost-effective online marketing strategies instead of expensive advertising.
- Join a Larger Firm First – Gain experience, save money, and transition into independence when financially ready.

**The Bottom Line**

While it's tempting to take out a loan and accelerate growth, most financial advisors are better off financing their business with time, not debt. The stress of loan payments, reduced flexibility, and long-term financial burden often outweigh the benefits of quick capital.

☑ Start lean. Grow strategically. Avoid debt.
☑ Let revenue, not loans, fund your expansion.
☑ Focus on building relationships and delivering value—success will follow.

And frankly, this should be your first test as a financial advisor. Work on your own plan first. If you can't plan out your own finances, perhaps you don't have the mindset to handle other people's finances, or you should just work for a larger firm. But if you really want to be good at giving financial advice, you should be good at taking your own advice first. Apply what you've learned to yourself and your practice and you'll be able to relate it better to clients.

But there is an exception to my recommendation to not borrow money to build a practice. The exception comes in the form of buying a book of business from another advisor or firm. This is much harder than people think, but it can work if a few guidelines are followed:

The primary thing to consider when buying a book is the math must work. This includes the debt payment, and ongoing income for the buyer as they will not have time to prospect for new advisors. And this option is better for advisors who are not as proficient at selling to new clients, but might have a more personable, service minded, or technical approach to their practice. In this case, the business model is completely different. It must be evaluated from a perspective of valuation of the practice based on:

1) Personality and communication styles of buyer and seller. If this isn't completely aligned from the beginning, nothing else matters. The clients will not remain with the new advisor. It may take a year or two for them to become unhappy, but they'll eventually leave to find someone they can communicate with.
2) Average age of the clients. If the average age of the book of business for sale is over 75 or older, it's safe to assume the clients will not be there long enough to cover any type of long-term amortization of the debt. And I've heard many sellers say the age is not an issue because they, "have great relationships with the next generation and the money will stay

after the clients pass away". This might be true for some small portion of the assets, but it's risky to borrow money based on that assumption. And in my experience, this doesn't work because the next generation has a different plan for the money, and they likely didn't tell their parent about it.

3) Familiarity with the existing service model. Many advisors believe they can "sell" their model to the clients in the book they are buying. It doesn't make any sense to buy a book of business and then must resell yourself with a different service than the clients are used to. You'll already have a challenge in selling yourself to the clients, don't add another hurdle by adding a different product or service to the mix.
4) Geographic location is an issue. If the clients have worked with their advisor remotely, they'll be comfortable with doing it again. As most clients with investable assets are older, they are likely more used to meeting in person. And if they are told they need to go to a different city to meet their advisor, it's not likely to last for long. In my experience, the higher probability for a successful transition exists when the buyer moves into the seller's office space and takes over the lease. It's best to minimize the obstacles for the clients to retain them.
5) Fee or revenue available to service debt. This is a simple issue, but it's often overlooked as advisors are too anxious to buy a practice. And I've seen sellers demand that the buyers "work for free" for a few years to pay off the debt in a short period of time. Again, this is another challenge as the buyer has the opportunity cost of not being able to bring on new clients while they are transitioning the purchased book of business and servicing those people. And if just a few clients chose to leave the practice, the buyer is immediately upside-down regarding cash flow.
6) Seller must keep some skin in the game. Not much, and not for long, but if the seller isn't willing to stay through the transition, it's a sign that the practice isn't as strong as they are representing. And the seller might even agree to keep a monetary incentive for a successful transition. They should do this if their representations are accurate.

Buying a book of business seems like the answer for many advisors struggling to build a practice. Here are a few examples I've seen or been involved in over the years.

Here's an example. We found a practice in the Outer Banks that was for sale. The math worked on a $1 million purchase price, and the culture seemed to be a good fit. We drove 7 hours to meet with the sellers and talk through all the details, and everything was going well. We had already determined we were going to open a local office in the same town to service those clients. But during our due diligence, we found out there was one client that represented almost 25% of the revenue of the book, and this client was in his mid-eighties. We were assured by the seller this client was committed to keeping his investments with the firm and his children would do the same. But it's a lot of money to invest on a simple hope that these representations would come true. Anything can happen, and that issue alone is why we walked away from it.

Another example is when one of my partners was friends with another advisor in our city, who suddenly passed away. As any good friend would do, my partner stepped in and tried to maintain the practice for the benefit of the family. He determined a value for the practice and committed to paying the family over the next few years as he assumed the client relationships. As my partner began the painstaking work of meeting with the clients, learning their needs and giving some income to the family of the deceased advisor, it quickly became apparent that all the clients were sold annuities in which all the commission was taken upfront. While the financial statements for the practice verified good revenue, it all came from commission from products that had no recurring revenue. And by getting the accounts assigned over to my partner, he then had to service these accounts for years without the benefit of getting paid for it. Because my partner is an ethical person and would have done this to help the widow regardless, it still worked out. But for anyone looking to buy that practice, the financial statements would have been deceiving.

Being an advisor is tough! There are many aspects to master, especially when you are the only one responsible for the success of your practice. And you need to be good at many things at the same time. This means you must:

· Plan Your Time – Time is the most valuable resource for any financial advisor. Effective time management ensures that advisors focus on high-impact activities like client meetings, prospecting, and continuing education. This includes setting daily priorities, blocking time for deep work, and eliminating distractions.

· Plan Your Money – Financial advisors must practice what they preach. Managing both personal and business finances effectively is crucial. This means budgeting for marketing, technology, and staff while ensuring personal financial security through savings and investments.

· Plan Your Work – Success doesn't happen by accident. Advisors need a structured business plan outlining their target market, client acquisition strategies, service model, and long-term goals. Without a plan, it's easy to waste time on unproductive tasks.

· Work Your Plan – Execution is everything. Once a plan is in place, consistency and discipline are required to follow through. This means sticking to prospecting schedules, delivering value to clients, and continuously refining strategies based on result

## CHAPTER 6

# What Type of Advisor Do You Want to Be When You Grow Up?

The financial advising industry is incredibly diverse, with multiple business models, compensation structures, and client service approaches. As a young advisor, finding the right fit early on can make all the difference in your career trajectory. Do you want to build a high-revenue firm, prioritize service over profit, or focus on giving back to your community? Or would you prefer the security of working with a larger firm that shares the responsibility, the risk, and the referrals to grow your practice?

This chapter will help you define your path by exploring different business models, client strategies, and the foundational decisions that shape your practice.

Revenue-Oriented, Service-Oriented, or Community-Oriented?

Before diving into the mechanics of running a practice, take a step back and define your motivations.

- Revenue-Oriented – Your goal is to build a highly profitable business. You focus on growth, efficiency, and high-net-worth clients.
- Team-Oriented – You want to build and work in a team environment where each person handles a different aspect of the practice.
- Service-Oriented – You prioritize personalized service, deep

relationships, and client experience, often over rapid expansion.

- Community-Oriented – You focus on serving a niche market or a specific community, possibly at the expense of higher margins.
- Lifestyle Practice – You focus on just enough clients to make a good living but must struggle with small business issues and compliance while have a great work life balance.
- Scalable business model – You want to build a strong firm and grow it with multiple advisors and a well-known company platform.

Understanding where you fit on this spectrum will help you make better decisions about your business model, pricing, and client relationships. It will also help you determine if you want to work for another firm or start your own at some point.

Laying Out Your Growth Plan

Success doesn't happen by accident. A clear growth plan gives you direction and helps you stay accountable. Consider:

- What's your five-year vision? How big do you want your practice to be?
- What are your revenue goals? How many clients do you need to reach them?
- What's your client acquisition strategy? Networking, digital marketing, referrals?
- How will you measure success? Revenue? Client retention? Work-life balance?

Write it down. A vague idea is just a dream. A written plan is a roadmap, regardless of where you work.

Determining Your Tech Stack. Technology can either be your biggest advantage or your biggest headache. Invest in tools that help you:

- Manage client relationships (CRM)
- Track investments and performance
- Automate marketing and client communication-really important

- Streamline compliance and operations
- Client portals
- Social media monitoring and sales content

Don't get overwhelmed by flashy software—choose tech that fits your workflow and enhances productivity and operations.

Success in financial advising isn't just about knowledge—it's about execution. Structure your work with a spreadsheet or digital tool that sets clear goals and tracks activities. One of the biggest issues is the follow up of the details. After every client meeting or phone call, there will be follow up items. And the details matter. It's how the clients know you are doing what you said you will do. Advisors must have a strategy for how they do this. And the strategy can vary from using post it notes to inputting everything in a CRM

Time-Blocking: Work Your Plan

Breaking your day into structured time blocks keeps you from getting distracted and ensures you're making consistent progress. Here's a proven framework:

1. Marketing & social media – Engage with prospects, create content, and build your brand.
2. Client Meetings & Prep – Deliver value, not just reports. Be prepared and intentional.
3. Emails – Set dedicated times to manage communications to avoid constant distractions.
4. Investments – Stay informed, analyze portfolios, and strategize for clients.
5. Operations – Handle paperwork, back-office tasks, and streamline processes.
6. Compliance – Stay on top of regulatory requirements to avoid legal headaches.
7. Business Growth/Review – Regularly check your progress against your goals and adjust.

The key to growth isn't doing more—it's doing the right things consistently.

## Planning Your Client Base: Identify Who You WANT to Work With

Not all clients are created equal. The sooner you define your ideal client, the faster you'll build a business that fits your vision.

### What's Your Niche?

Successful advisors specialize. Do you want to work with:

- Executives?
- Business owners?
- Doctors and professionals?
- Young families?
- Retirees?

Your niche will shape your marketing, service model, and expertise.

### Focus on Your Value Proposition

Why should clients choose you over another advisor? Your value prop should be clear, specific, and meaningful. It's not just "I help people retire." It's how you help them.

### Define Your Ideal Client's Personality

Forget about net worth for a moment. Who do you enjoy working with?

- Do they value advice or just chase returns?
- Do they respect your time and expertise?
- Are they engaged in their financial future?

Defining this now will save you years of frustration with the wrong clients.

## Who Should You Surround Yourself With?

The saying "surround yourself with people better than you" isn't entirely true. Instead, surround yourself with people you trust—people you can learn from, collaborate with, and rely on.

- Mentors who've been where you want to go
- Peers who challenge and support you
- Team members who complement your weaknesses

Success in financial advising isn't a solo game. Build a strong network early.

## Figure Out Your Communication Style—Then Own It

How you communicate with clients is just as important as what you know. Find a style that fits you, own it, and sell it.

1. Own Your Mistakes – Client's respect honesty. A well-handled mistake can strengthen trust. (Insert story: A time you admitted a mistake and how it built credibility.)
2. Ask Clients for Help—Not Referrals – Instead of saying, "Do you know anyone who could use my services?", say, "I'm trying to build relationships with people like you. How do you think I should go about that?"

Personal note: When I started my practice, I asked 5 people to help me. They were not all clients, but they were people whose opinions I respected and who I thought were interested in helping me succeed.

I set up an advisory board and took the group to dinner once a month to ask for guidance and help. My business model was to limit the number of clients I could serve to 100 families. These folks loved the model. And before long, they too were emotionally invested in my success. I never had to ask for their business, I just asked them to help me, and every one of them agreed they wanted to help. And several pulled me aside to confirm they would be "one of the 100 clients"!

After several months of growth, dinner discussions, planning on service models and communication, we were about to wrap up our last meeting. I was so thankful for these folks and their willingness to spend time helping me. As we ended the meeting, one person pulled me aside and told me she was proud of what I was doing. Then she told me something I'll never forget. She told me my logo was terrible and that I needed to hire a professional to develop a new logo. I was not offended at all but quickly recognized how much she was helping me. I trusted her opinion, so I quickly hired a marketing person and developed a new logo, which we still have today.

This group of people not only helped me build the business model, but they also helped give me the confidence to step out on my own, and they were my safety net. I'm forever grateful.

3. Take a Personal Interest – Clients don't remember financial plans. They remember personal connections. Show up to their events, send handwritten notes, or do one thing they'll never forget.

Personal Note: I think it's important to do one thing for every client, that they'll never forget. This can be as simple as showing up for a birthday party or helping them buy a car. These things show that you care, and they'll never forget it.

Find Resources to Fill in the Weaknesses. No advisor is great at everything. Recognizing your weaknesses early allows you to:

- Partner with specialists (tax, legal, investments)
- Gain credibility through strategic collaborations
- Focus on your strengths while outsourcing other areas

As you start your journey, remember there's no single "right way" to be an advisor. The best path is the one that fits your strengths, values, and vision. Define your niche. Work your plan. Build meaningful relationships. The rest will follow.

# CHAPTER 7

# Sales – the most important thing! Is it really?

Success in financial advising depends on the ability to sell—but not in the way most people think. You're not selling products, stock picks, or financial plans. You're selling trust, expertise, and solutions to problems clients care about.

Many young advisors struggle with the idea of selling because they associate it with pushing products. But the best salespeople don't feel like salespeople at all. They're problem-solvers, educators, and trusted partners. This chapter will break down how to approach sales the right way—ethically, effectively, and without turning clients off.

The first thing you'll have to determine is your growth strategy. There are many aspects to determining your path for this. The main factor is cashflow and how much you are willing to invest into your practice for growth.

Sales Strategies

We won't cover this in depth because entire books have been written about this process alone. And they are all correct. But none of them will work for a new advisor until each advisor spends time on their own business plan. This isn't just important as a business owner, it's crucial and is an absolute necessity.

To do this, you'll need to know a few things that you won't yet have good data to input into your business plan. But you can start with a few assumptions and adjust as you gain more experience.

First, what is the average account size you are most comfortable with? Many advisors will say they want to work with big accounts. This is big mistake if you don't have experience with this type of client. Their needs are higher, their expectation of your knowledge is higher, and frankly, the fees are lower per AUM. Advisors must start with client demographics they are familiar with. And if you don't know, start with averages below $250k and build your model from there.

Next, how many families with this average account size, do you need in your first year? This is completely dependent on your growth goals and your capacity. Of course, everyone thinks they can bring on 100 clients per year. This means you haven't really thought through your long-term plan, your onboarding process, investment model, or your service model. I could argue that 100 clients are the max that every advisor should have…

Then, once that you've decided to add X number of clients each year, what's your closing ratio? Again, every advisor thinks the ratio is 75-100%. When you are starting out, your closing ratio is more like 25%. And if you are buying leads or networking, the average closing ratio is about 5%.

Now do the math. If your average account size is "A", and you need "B" number of families with "C" closing ratio, you'll need to get in front of a bunch of prospects to get to this number. But now you know exactly how many prospects you need. Now you just need to determine how to find them. But you can hold yourself accountable each month to reach your growth goal, much like a financial plan for a client.

Do this math every year as your statistics will change. But it's important that you know these numbers and adjust them accordingly. Once you have this information, it's easier to adjust your business plan to determine how you are going to generate these leads.

You should also consider your selling style, and the type of clients you want to sell to. Some advisors like the chase and the sales process. I prefer to meet with clients, provide a solution to their problem, primarily through a financial plan, and then let them decide if I'm the right guy to solve the problem for them. I've never been good at sales, but I'm good at addressing the clients' concerns, which ultimately leads to the sale. But you must understand how you like to sell and identify a process for this once you've identified a prospect.

Lead Generation comes down to 3 things, time, money, and process.

Anyone can generate leads if they have enough time. I've met many advisors who still knock on doors. It's tough, and it's a numbers game, but you'll get in your daily exercise. Maybe it works, maybe not, but it'll give you experience in talking to people. But putting time into lead generation can also take the form of networking, cold calling, of just building a COI list using advisory boards, volunteer activities etc. This is the long way of working through the lead generation process. And if you don't already have an established network to contact, this will take many years to build. It works, but it's a difficult path, and spending the time to build it means you must have the financial patience to be able to last in this business with minimal income.

The other way to generate leads is to spend money. There are many lead generation tools available. Most of them rely on social media contacts but some also spend money on your behalf to attract leads. Some of these tool's work, and I've seen a few advisors build viable practices this way. But it's expensive, and you must budget the marketing dollars for at least a year. And when you do this, you must add the cost variable into your practice equation of A times B equals C which costs D per lead. And with an average closing ratio of 5%, you can see how this gets expensive quickly. But it works if you've chosen the right lead generation tool.

Whether you decide to spend the time or the money, neither works without a planning process for how to implement these things. Too many advisors want to jump out and start a practice because they believe the old philosophy of "build it and they will come". The lack of a plan for how to get there translates into many hungry years of wondering why the practice hasn't grown much. And frankly, we are financial planners. This exercise for our practice is no different than the financial plan we do for our clients. We need to practice what we preach, build out a plan, and stick to it.

In most cases, the buildout of the plan incorporates time and money into the process. This is the formula that will yield the most success. And once you have the formula, you are ready to determine how you relate to clients and prospects.

You should also identify some good sales and marketing resources, and ironically, some of your clients and prospects are the absolute best options for this. As you build your practice, ask your clients for help. Don't ask them for referrals. But your clients want to take a personal interest in your success. And they want to know about your practice.

Personal experience – when I started my practice, I worked with a handful of clients every month for a few months to help shape my practice. I will always be grateful to this group for the guidance and direction they provided to me which ultimately built the foundation for our firm. But I'll never forget one instance, where a client came up to me after our final meeting. She told me she loved everything I was doing to build a practice and was pleased to be part of it. Then she handed my business card back to me and said, "You have got to change this logo. It's terrible and you need something more professional!" It was a little shocking, but it was great advice, for which I acted upon immediately. And she was right.

Here are a few things to keep in mind

Clients and Prospects Do NOT Want to Meet with You. Let's be honest—clients aren't waking up in the morning excited about meeting with a financial advisor. Many of them already know they don't have enough money, are behind on retirement, or aren't making the best financial decisions. And many aren't happy with their current advisor, so why would they want to take the risk of meeting with another one they might not like. They don't want to sit in a conference room and be told what they already know.

Your first job is to make them comfortable. That means:
✓ Meeting in an environment where they feel at ease, talking about things they understand. Don't use acronyms. It makes clients feel like you are talking over their head.
✓ Focusing on them, not your agenda. Ask them questions, it'll put them at ease.
✓ Starting with what they care about, not what you want to talk about.

Let Them Talk. One of the biggest mistakes new advisors make is talking too much. You want to prove you know your stuff, but the more you talk, the less they trust you. Clients need to feel heard. The more they talk, the more comfortable they'll be.

Golden rule: Do NOT interrupt. Ever. Many advisors feel the urge to jump in and demonstrate expertise. Don't. Interrupting signals that you care more about what you know than what they need.

Instead, practice active listening:

- Nod and acknowledge what they're saying
- Repeat back key points
- Ask follow-up questions
- Let them finish their thoughts

You don't gain trust by proving how smart you are—you gain trust by listening. I've seen many young advisors spend time interrupting prospects or clients to interject a point they are trying to make. It comes from a place of insecurity, and the advisor is trying to demonstrate their industry knowledge and solve a problem immediately. In reality, the client will be insulted if they are constantly interrupted, and the lines of communication will die an early death.

Over-Communicate—But Make It Personal. People don't relate to stock market charts or economic forecasts. They relate to stories.

- Start with small talk. Find a common interest.
- Look for a personal nugget—something you can connect on.
- Use relatable examples rather than industry jargon.

The more human you are, the more comfortable they'll be. Tell lots of stories about yourself and things you have in common. It lets them get to know you. But keep coming back to them and their issues or concerns. It's why they are there.

Solve Their Immediate Problem FIRST. We've all heard:

☝ "Clients don't care how much you know until they know how much you care." It's not just a saying—it's reality.

You might know that a client's real issue isn't their credit card debt but their lack of long-term savings. But if their biggest concern is paying off that debt, that's where you start.

- ◇ Solve their immediate problem.
- ◇ Then, guide them to the bigger issues.
- ◇ Help them understand how everything connects.

Your role isn't to dictate—it's to guide.

Avoid Jargon—Nobody Cares About Your Cool Tech

Advisors love talking about:
✖ Market trends
✖ Investment screens
✖ The fancy technology they use

Clients? They don't care. We can talk about those things all day long. But you'll see them glaze over within 10 minutes of an advisor trying to prove how smart they are. The clients are at the meeting to talk about their issues, not the advisors' issues.

Using jargon doesn't make you look smart—it makes you unrelatable.

Keep things simple:
✓ Instead of "asset allocation," say "diversifying your investments."
✓ Instead of "volatility," say "ups and downs of the market."
✓ Instead of "equities," say "stocks."

You don't need to sound like a finance professor. Just sound like a human.

Don't "Fake It 'Til You Make It". Too many young advisors believe they need to look successful to gain trust. Expensive suits, fancy watches, luxury cars—it's all an illusion. Clients don't care if you drive an Italian sports car. They care that you understand them.

- ◇ If they're struggling, show them you understand their struggle.
- ◇ If they're uncertain, reassure them with honesty.
- ◇ If they're overwhelmed, break things down into simple steps.

Authenticity is better than flashy appearances every time.

Embrace Technology—But Don't Hide Behind It. Technology is a powerful tool, but it should never replace real conversations.

✓ Use tech to enhance your practice, not as a crutch
✓ Automate tasks, but don't automate relationships
✓ Clients want a human connection, not just an app

The best advisors use technology efficiently while keeping interactions personal. This is becoming increasingly difficult as technology and AI change the sales landscape. Advisors can no longer build a strong practice based on their network and social skills alone. The use of digital tools is now a requirement to grow and manage a practice. You should always be thinking of how to best use the tools that are available but use them in a way that makes you stand out from all the other advisors who are using the same tools. Uniqueness, specificity, and creativity are the things that make the technology work better and draw focus to your practice. Technology is just the accelerator for it.

Rethink How You Attract Clients. Traditional advisors rely on **referrals, networking events, and cold calling**—methods that work but are increasingly outdated. Instead, consider:

☑ **Creating Educational Content:**

- Start a **YouTube channel, podcast, or blog** where you simplify financial topics for a specific audience (e.g., young professionals, business owners, or retirees).
- Offer free guides, checklists, or webinars to build an email list of potential clients.
- Take informational articles to your referral sources. Give them a copy and ask them if it might help some of their clients.
- Offer to help your referral sources personally. Maybe they need a financial plan or investment advice. You can give them some things for free that demonstrate your willingness to help, your knowledge, and that you care.

☑ **Hosting Online Events Instead of In-Person Seminars:**

- Run monthly virtual Q&A sessions on Zoom or LinkedIn Live, making it easier for busy clients to attend.
- Partner with other professionals (CPAs, attorneys, real estate agents) for cross-promotion.

☑ **Using social media the Right Way:**

- Share insights, personal stories, and client success examples (without violating compliance).
- Engage in conversations—don't just post generic financial tips.
- Use LinkedIn to connect with professionals who **need an advisor** instead of just networking with other advisors.

☑ **Automating Lead Generation:**

- Create a simple **email drip campaign** to nurture leads instead of following up manually with every prospect.

- Use paid ads on social media targeted at a specific audience (e.g., "High-income professionals needing tax-efficient retirement strategies").

Sales Isn't About Selling—It's About Serving

If you:
☑ Listen first
☑ Make clients comfortable
☑ Solve real problems
☑ Communicate simply
☑ Stay authentic

You won't have to "sell" at all—clients will want to work with you. And that's what real success looks like in this business.

Let's discuss buying leads vs networking as sales tools. Both strategies are viable and can work. They can also both fail due to the time invested or focusing on the wrong places. Anyone can spend money on marketing, but it does not guarantee success. In today's world, there are marketing and lead generation tools all over social media. If you don't believe me, just enter "lead generation" in a search engine one time, and you'll see the ads forever! But it's easy to go broke trying to "buy" business.

For example, if you get in front of 10 appointments per week as leads that you bought, yet you don't know how to speak to them, or don't have the network of resources to use for your discussions, then the time and the money is wasted. This is where the network comes in. Once you start having meetings with other financial, accounting, or legal professionals who can provide ancillary services to your clients, it will be easier for you to have well rounded discussions and help solve some of your client's immediate needs.

I've seen advisors who stay in their office with the door closed so they can just call leads all day. It can work from a volume perspective, but it lacks depth of knowledge, team relationships, and is socially awkward. I've also seen advisors who spend all their time networking and not enough time generating leads. This is the most fun way to build a practice if you are socially motivated, but it's also the slowest way to do it. Advisors must have a goal for how many appointments they need in a month, and then execute the plan with technology, lead generation, and networking to accomplish the goal.

Another hurdle for newer advisors who are prospecting is the fear of being told "NO". This should never be taken as a judgement on your personality, your sales style, or your ability as an advisor. Remember that clients only move to a new advisor when they have an issue with the prior one. If there's no issue, they likely won't move to you, regardless of how good you are. So, you'll need to stay in front of them for years, until there is an issue with their current advisor. But, when they say "No" to moving their accounts, it's a good thing!

1) It's one less prospect on your list that you must waste time wondering about. Take them off the list and add them to a drip campaign. This gives you more time to focus on folks that might say "Yes".
2) This industry is a numbers game. Every advisor will get some percentage of "Nos" for every "Yes". Every time someone tells you NO, you are that much closer to getting a "Yes".
3) Someone telling you NO, is something you MUST get comfortable with. It's part of the process and makes you better for the next prospect you speak with.

On the flip side, it's also OK for us to say "NO" to taking on a new client. There are many cases where we just cannot help them. Maybe their expenses exceed their cash flow, or they don't have any assets to manage. Or frankly, perhaps your personalities don't mesh or they expect too much. You should always have the confidence in yourself to tell them if it's not a good fit. This will save many hours of stress in the future. And it may limit your liability, especially if there's a conflict over a miscommunication.

However, I do NOT think it's OK to tell someone "No" due to account size, especially early in our careers. It's incumbent on us to help everyone we can help if we can make a difference and we like working with that person or family. And early on, we need the experience, the exposure to potential referrals, and the network. And sometimes, you can make a bigger difference for folks with smaller account balances by making a just a few adjustments to things they don't understand.

On the other side, as your career progresses, it's ok to NOT take a client due to time constraints or personality conflicts, especially if you are limiting your growth and have too many clients. In these specific scenarios, you are helping the clients by declining to take them if there is a risk of you providing poor service or inadequate communication.

The Benefits of Selling the Right Way

1. You Build Real Client Relationships. The best clients don't see you as just an advisor—they see you as family. The more they trust you, the more likely they are to refer others. Let them talk and find a common thread to discuss. This will put them at ease and confirm to them that you've been listening.

2. You Take on a Higher Level of Responsibility. When you approach sales with integrity, you own your role as a trusted guide. That means doing what's best for clients—not what makes you the most money. Clients and prospects will sense this every time.

3. You Build Value in Your Practice. A strong book of loyal clients = a valuable business. Firms and buyers don't just look at how many clients you have—they look at how deep those relationships are.

4. It Encourages Excellence, Not Mediocrity. Advisors who rely on sales gimmicks or shortcuts don't last. The ones who focus on service and relationships do. Great sales aren't just about closing deals—they're about keeping clients. And sales is purely a volume game. You must get comfortable with being told NO. If this makes you uncomfortable, you should work for an advisor who is comfortable with this and buy their practice later.

5. Remember that clients need us when they have a need, not when we ask them to do business with us. This presents the problem of

either staying in touch with our network, so they'll think of us when they have a need, or we must use technology to find clients that have the need immediately. And how do we find those people? It's a tough process that requires building the right network and adopting technology at the same time.

As we wrap up this chapter, we've discussed some of the different aspects of the sales process. Is this really the most important thing to determine success? I think it is, if you keep it in perspective. It's the most important aspect regarding your success, but that is defined differently by every advisor. Success might be defined by a specific income goal or by a specific number of families in the practice. But it's also defined by the relationships you build within your practice. As I've said before, the people you work with should be clients you identify with, respect, and enjoy working with. Sure, early in our practice growth, we must be more open minded about the clients we accept, primarily from a revenue perspective. But as the practice grows, the sales focus evolves from quantity to quality. It's just not always about volume. Always keep the long-term goals in mind and work towards it. The sales are critical, but how you do the sales, who you do the sales for, and how you build relationships are just as important.

# CHAPTER 8

# Servicing – The Key to Retention and Referrals

Once you've built a great practice and have mastered all your sales and marketing skills, you'll need to implement a gradual shift away from being the sales guru. And you'll have to learn how to execute in a service environment to retain all the clients you spent years recruiting. This goes well beyond sales, where exceptional client service is what keeps your business thriving. Retention isn't just about managing investments—it's about making clients feel valued, informed, and understood. A great service model turns satisfied clients into lifelong advocates who refer others to you.

This chapter covers the fundamentals of providing outstanding client service, managing expectations, and implementing systems that ensure long-term engagement. We'll also discuss how technology and AI can enhance the client experience—rather than replace human advisors.

## Client Service Isn't Rocket Science

Most advisors believe they know how to service clients, but they forget basic concepts. Sometimes this is a simple concept that is overlooked. For example, if an advisor spends years in sales to build a practice, how do they transition to servicing clients. In my experience, they don't. Most advisors are good at sales, or they are good at service, but not both. As your practice grows, you must make a conscious effort to determine what you are good at or which part you'd like to focus on for success. If you enjoy the selling aspects, hire someone to help with the service. If you enjoy the service aspect more that the sales aspect, you'll need to focus on the transition to a service-based practice when your book of business reaches a particular size. Otherwise, your client will feel neglected as you get too busy to honor your commitments to them. Neither philosophy is wrong. And you'll determine which path you like early in the development of your practice.

Many advisors overcomplicate client service. It's not about elaborate reports, fancy dinners, or excessive meetings. It's about consistent communication and genuine care.

Define Your Client Service Model

◇ Clients need us on their schedule, not ours. Be flexible and available.

Many advisors operate on their own time, expecting clients to fit into their calendar. Flip that mindset. Don't be surprised if clients don't respond to your communications. But they'll reach out when THEY need something.

I've spent a few years being offended by this only to realize we work for them. We fill a need, but it's a periodic need, and may not be a personal friendship. But some turn into friendships.

✓ Be flexible—make time when clients need you.
✓ Offer multiple communication channels—some prefer emails, others like calls or video chats.
✓ Have proactive touchpoints—don't just reach out when there's a problem.

◇ Deal with their concerns first. If they're worried about something minor, address it before pushing long-term planning.
If a client is worried about something minor (like a single stock dropping in their portfolio), address it before discussing long-term planning.
✓ Clients need to feel heard.

✓ Once their immediate concerns are addressed, they'll be more receptive to broader discussions. Then they'll trust you enough to take your advice on things they need to hear about.

◇ Don't confuse "busyness" with business. If your schedule is packed with unnecessary tasks, reevaluate your priorities. And always keep politics and religion OUT of the discussions. This never ends well. Clients will frequently want to go there, but you must stay in the middle of this road and keep them on track. If they go down the rabbit hole, do not follow them. Stay focused on your professional task as their fiduciary.

Many advisors mistake being busy for being productive. Client service isn't about having more meetings—it's about having the right conversations. Client sales are about having more meetings. And distractions are about just answering emails, checking social media, and not being productive at any level. It's really important you don't confuse these three things.

✓ Focus on high-value interactions, not unnecessary tasks.
✓ Use technology to automate low-value work so you can focus on client relationships.

1. When you work in a client's account, send them a quick update.

    - It can be as simple as: "I just rebalanced your portfolio based on our last conversation. Let me know if you have any questions!"
    - Small touches like this show clients you're proactively managing their money.

2. Call them periodically—just to check in.

    - You don't need a reason. Just ask how they're doing.
    - Advisors often sit around discussing client situations with each other when they should be calling the client instead.

3. Follow up on personal details and help them WANT to meet with you.

- If a client mentioned their child was starting college, check in to ask how it's going.
- If they had a surgery scheduled, follow up with a "How are you feeling?"
- Make the meetings enjoyable. Now that they are clients, you can talk a little more. Tell them personal stories they'll relate to, be human and connect on a personal level.
- These small personal touches build relationships that go beyond financial advising.
- Do one thing for EVERY client, that's unexpected. Go to a birthday party, attend a retirement gathering, donate to their charity, help them buy a house or car. This will never be forgotten because no one else does it.

Here is a personal experience that relates to this theory. My longtime assistant and business partner helped me with an older married couple and their finances. They came into the office looking for a good investment for their annual tax contribution. Over the course of a few meetings and after they became comfortable with us, we determined they had accounts in at least 22 different financial institutions. When we initially asked them how much money they thought they had, the thought they had about $250-300,000. Over the next few months, my business partner helped them combine all the accounts into three accounts that we managed for them. So rather than them chasing the best CD rate for an annual IRA contribution, we handled it for them. And by the way, the total amount of money in the combined accounts was well over $1mm. But this wouldn't have happened had my partner not physically gone to the bank with the wife to help close out some of the accounts. This was above and beyond our jobs, but the clients needed the help.

Sadly, after we consolidated everything, the husband passed away suddenly and unexpectedly. But fortunately, all the assets were consolidated and accounted for. Had we not been involved or had my partner NOT gone to the bank to help close accounts; it may have taken years to gather all the accounts together.

But here is a word of caution that I've learned many times throughout my career. Be careful to NOT let your emotions make financial decisions for your closest clients. Here's what I mean.

We tell clients they need us to help prevent them from making emotional decision regarding their finances. Our job is to prevent them from making a big mistake they may never recover from, specifically relating to investing. Yet, as advisors, we all have close friends or family that we want to do a "great" job for or help overcome some financial hardship. And since we're in the business, we are smart enough to go outside of our normal processes, just this one time, to make a difference for someone we care about, right? That's entirely wrong. Clients need us because of our processes, procedures, and lack of emotional investing. If we change this philosophy for any of them, even just one, then we expose them to the emotional risk they hired us to avoid. When we add the emotional stress into our process, we become susceptible to the same risks the clients had without us. I've seen it happen, and it makes a tough situation even worse.

Embracing Technology, AI, and Practice Management. At a recent industry conference, I heard a few quotes that perfectly sum up the future of financial advising:

1. "AI WILL replace financial advisors. AI WILL NOT replace financial advisors who use AI."

Technology isn't something to fear—it's a tool to enhance your practice. Advisors who ignore AI will struggle to compete, but those who embrace it will provide better service, automate repetitive tasks, and free up more time for client relationships.

- Use AI for data analysis, investment research, and client segmentation.
- Automate scheduling, reminders, birthdays, and account alerts.
- Let AI assist with portfolio monitoring—but human relationships will always be the key to success.

2. Clients Don't Expect Us to Beat a Benchmark—They Expect Us to Beat Their Personal Returns.

Most clients don't care if you outperform the S&P 500. They care about:
✓ Whether they're on track for retirement
✓ Whether they feel financially secure
✓ Whether they can buy a vacation home, fund their child's education, or leave a legacy

Your job isn't to "win" against the market. It's to help clients win their personal financial game. You are on the same team.

3. Determine Your Software Suite Early—But Don't Overanalyze It. Then update it frequently.

Advisors can waste months selecting the "perfect" CRM, financial planning software, or portfolio management system. But technology evolves fast.

✓ Choose a solid foundation that fits your workflow.
✓ Learn it well enough to be efficient. But don't overthink it. Analysis paralysis is real.
✓ Move on to more important things—like serving clients.

Gathering Client Feedback: The Power of Surveys

Want to know if your service model is working? Ask your clients.

A simple annual client survey can give you invaluable insights. Here are key areas to focus on:

1. Trust

- Do clients feel confident in your guidance?
- Do they believe you always act in their best interest?

2. Communication

- Are you reaching out often enough?
- Do they feel comfortable contacting you with concerns?
- Do they understand their financial plan?

3. Account Performance Relative to Their Plan

- Are they happy with how their accounts are being managed?
- Do they feel like they're making progress toward their goals?

4. Planning & Education

- Are you helping them understand their financial future?
- Do they feel educated, or do they feel like they're in the dark?

5. Overall Financial Well-Being

- Do they feel less stressed about money because of your guidance?
- Are you helping them gain peace of mind, not just grow assets?

These survey responses can shape how you improve your service model and address blind spots before they become issues.

The Benefits of Exceptional Client Service

1. Stronger Client Relationships—They Become Your Family

When you genuinely care about clients, they'll stay with you for life—and introduce you to their family and friends.

2. A Higher Level of Responsibility & Trust

Great advisors don't just manage money—they guide major life decisions. Clients will rely on you beyond your investment expertise. They'll call you for everything, and they'll challenge you to be better. And I've heard many times from my clients, "I can talk to you about things I'm uncomfortable sharing with anyone else". That's because, if we do our job right, we will see all their confidential information and can be a sounding board for all their financial decisions. Many times, these discussions and close confidentiality are what turns average clients into great friends.

Here's a personal experience that relates to this theory. I took on a planning client who wanted to sell his business and retire. Over the course of several months, we talked strategy to sell the business, generate cash and explore the hobbies he wanted to pursue. But his wife NEVER came to a meeting, so I never met her. At the end of the planning process when I presented the financial numbers, this client needed an additional $300,000 to meet his income goal. When I showed him this problem, he simply said, "that's OK, I have that in cash that I keep in the walls of my workshop, but my wife doesn't know about it". You can see the issue that's starting to emerge.

At the end of the meeting, we agreed to meet again with his wife where I would simply state the shortfall and go through the plan. But he asked that I not discuss his hidden cash. He was going out of town for vacation and agreed to bring her into the office upon his return so we could begin the process for selling his business.

While on vacation the following week, my client was riding his snowmobile and hit a tree. He passed away in the hills of Michigan with his son doing the things they loved, but it was a tragic and premature life event. And as you can see, the retirement plan was never fully implemented.

I then had the extremely awkward task of calling his wife, whom I had never met, to request that she tear open the walls of her deceased husband's workshop, to look for the cash. Fortunately, he had told her about me and the financial plan he was working on, and she found my business card on his desk, so she knew I was legitimate when I called within a few days of his passing. She immediately went to the workshop, found the cash, and called me back to say she was headed to the bank with it.

I spent the next several months helping her sell the business, pay off debts, and execute an alternate retirement plan. She was able to move out of state to be close to her children and was forever thankful for my help. Had he not told me about it, the cash would still be hidden in the walls.

3. Increased Practice Value & Business Growth

A well-serviced book of business isn't just rewarding—it's valuable.
✓ High client retention = Higher business valuation
✓ Happy clients = More referrals = Faster growth

4. It Does NOT Encourage Mediocrity

Advisors who focus only on sales tend to hit a plateau. Advisors who master service keep growing because they deliver real value.

Reinvent the Client Experience

Many financial advisors follow the same playbook for onboarding clients, presenting plans, and managing relationships. Instead of blending in, consider:

☑ Offering Multiple Service Models:

- Instead of charging solely on AUM (Assets Under Management), introduce:
  - Flat fees for financial planning (great for younger professionals).
  - Subscription-based services for ongoing financial coaching.
  - Project-based pricing (e.g., one-time retirement plans or investment audits).

☑ Gamify Financial Planning:

- Use interactive tools to help clients visualize their financial future.
- Try budgeting and investment simulators or gamified goal-setting apps.
- Create a personalized dashboard where clients can track their financial progress.

☑ Improve Communication & Accessibility:

- Offer text-based check-ins for quick updates instead of long emails or scheduled meetings.
- Use short video messages to explain complex financial strategies.
- Allow clients to book appointments through an online scheduling system instead of back-and-forth emails.

But we should also discuss a few pitfalls that I've seen over the last 3 decades.

Service Is the Real Sales Strategy

If you:
☑ Communicate consistently
☑ Solve problems proactively
☑ Use technology efficiently
☑ Build trust through genuine relationships

You won't have to "sell" anything—clients will want to stay, and they'll bring others with them.

Exceptional service isn't a bonus—it's the foundation of a thriving advisory practice.

# CHAPTER 9

# Using AI as the Independent Advisor's Leverage

The financial services industry has always evolved alongside technological advancements. From the invention of the ticker tape to online trading platforms and reasoning machines, each leap forward has reshaped how advisors serve their clients as AI reads, writes, reasons, and increasingly acts on behalf of its users with the use of specialized agents. Today, we stand at the edge of another industry shift. AI is not just a buzzword or a cool tool for large tech firms. It is fundamentally changing the way wealth management works, from how portfolios are built to how advisors engage with clients, and how advisors build a practice.

In this chapter, we explore the most significant changes AI is bringing to the wealth management industry, and how advisors can embrace these changes to thrive, not just survive.

Lead Generation and Practice Growth

I've already spoken about many basic ways to build a practice in other chapters. Those are fundamental practice structures that must be embraced and implemented. They will build your network and provide resources for you and your clients. And to enhance practice growth, advisors can "buy leads" through many marketing services who focus specifically on the wealth management industry. All these process work, but as a practice grows and scales up, there will be better ways to do this internally using AI.

The primary barrier to using AI for lead generation is cost. The setup fees and the sequence generation can get expensive to design. And if advisors don't have a basic knowledge of how to market themselves in a way that sets them apart from other advisors, the use of AI for marketing purposes is less impactful.

However, once you build the AI tool for long term lead generation, it should pay dividends regarding the marketing and growth of a practice. Think of it as a "pay now" or "pay later" concept. For example, if you simply buy leads, the cost is lower initially, which is why most advisors chose this path. With a lower monthly cost and a recurring monthly expense that can easily be included in a budget, the path is simple. And it's effective for sustainable practice growth.

With the use of AI, this initial investment is significantly higher initially as the systems or platform must be designed and built. Think of the costs as setup fees. Then there is the monthly "ad spend" in addition to the setup fees. The ad spend alone is typically more than the monthly cost to buy leads, so it's easy to see how this gets expensive quickly. But the difference is the amount and the type of leads generated. If buying leads generates a specific amount of leads each month, the AI platform should generate more leads every month and continually modify the type of leads received. This is the whole point of AI. And while it's theoretical and somewhat untested currently, there are many companies working on these models in varying sizes and platforms. Some use social media for conversational marketing while others push out content marketing through financial publications to build a "call to action" for the leads. The most effective campaign is a combination of all the above. And the bigger firms are adopting it quickly, which means they'll grab clients quicker than individual advisors who can't afford it.

Hyper-Personalized Financial Planning

Traditional financial planning often relies on static assumptions and broad client categories. AI, however, allows for a truly customized approach. By analyzing massive amounts of client data—spending habits, financial goals, life events, even behavioral cues—AI can generate financial plans that adjust dynamically. But it can also simplify the daily tasks associated with planning such as developing meeting briefs, plan narratives, client letters, and review agendas. AI can draft these things, but the advisor still owns it.

Imagine a client receives a job offer in a new city. An AI-powered planning platform could immediately recalculate the impact of relocation costs, housing changes, and income shifts on their retirement timeline and investment strategy. No need to wait for the next quarterly meeting. This level of personalization will soon become the expectation, not the exception.

Further, AI can analyze not just structured financial data but also unstructured data like emails, social media activity, or spending behaviors to anticipate needs clients may not even have voiced yet. For example, if a client begins browsing for college tuition information or posts about having a child, the system can suggest new planning modules or alert the advisor.

Advisors who adopt AI tools for planning will be able to deliver smarter, faster, and more relevant advice. Those who don't may find themselves outpaced by both machines and more tech-savvy competitors.

Smarter Investment Management

Robo-advisors were the first public face of AI in investment management, but that was just the beginning. Now, AI is enabling real-time risk assessment, automated portfolio rebalancing, and predictive analytics that spot opportunities and threats before they make headlines.

And on a daily basis, AI can do all the deep research on products and investments, research tax questions and planning scenarios and actually apply the "trust but verify rule" in real applications.

For example, AI can analyze global news, economic data, and market sentiment to adjust portfolios automatically—all while aligning with the client's risk profile and objectives. It doesn't sleep, it doesn't forget, and it isn't subject to emotional bias.

It also democratizes access to advanced strategies. Previously, techniques like factor investing, tax-loss harvesting, and scenario testing were reserved for high-net-worth individuals. AI can now bring those tools to everyday investors with lower fees and faster implementation, especially for those clients with looking for higher levels of sophistication.

Does that mean human advisors are obsolete? Far from it. But it does mean advisors need to redefine their value. Portfolio construction alone is no longer the differentiator. Instead, clients look to their advisor for guidance, context, and coaching—especially when AI flags a concern that requires a human touch.

Operational Efficiency

Chapter 1 already discussed the fact that 60% of an advisor's job is administrative follow up. AI is the first technology that attacks that burden directly-which matters the most to independent advisors because they don't have additional staff to handle these tasks like banks and wire houses. Behind the scenes, AI is streamlining operations in dramatic ways. Manual data entry, compliance paperwork, onboarding forms—these tasks are increasingly handled by intelligent automation.

For example, AI can drive the meeting intelligence by recording, summarizing, extracting follow ups, and populating the CRM with all the data.

This allows advisors and their teams to focus more on strategic conversations and less on administrative burdens. It also means firms can scale more easily, serving more clients without necessarily expanding headcount.

In addition, AI tools are enhancing compliance and regulatory oversight. By flagging potential issues automatically and keeping meticulous records, firms reduce their risk of errors or violations.

Firms using AI-driven onboarding platforms can complete KYC (Know Your Customer) and AML (Anti-Money Laundering) checks in minutes, not days.

Advisors who resist automation risk being bogged down by inefficiency, while those who embrace it gain time, energy, and bandwidth to deepen client relationships and grow their practices. But it's not an easy transition. Learning new software platforms is a daunting task. And when an advisor's time is stretched thin already, finding time to upgrade technology tools can be difficult.

Client Communication and Engagement

AI-powered communication tools are reshaping client service. Chatbots can answer common questions around the clock. Natural language processing tools can summarize meeting notes and suggest follow-up actions. Voice assistants can schedule appointments or pull up client files on command.

These technologies are not about replacing human interaction; they're about enhancing it. When the basics are handled by AI, advisors can be more present and attentive during meaningful conversations.

Imagine a system that listens to a recorded meeting and prompts the advisor to follow up on a client's birthday, concern about market volatility, or a mention of a new grandchild. These personalized touches, powered by AI, help foster trust and loyalty.

Going forward, clients will expect a seamless blend of digital convenience and human connection. Advisors who deliver both will stand out in an increasingly crowded field.

Behavioral Insights

Perhaps one of AI's most powerful (and underappreciated) capabilities is its ability to understand behavior. By analyzing patterns in client decisions, communication styles, and even tone of voice, AI can identify emotional states and behavioral risks. This is what advisors do for clients over a period of years. Now AI can do it over a period of days. But who determines if it's accurate? The advisor does.

For example, if a client starts logging into their account more frequently or selling off positions during market dips, the AI system may detect signs of fear or stress. It can alert the advisor, who can then reach out to provide reassurance and education. And it's difficult for AI to field a phone call when things come up unexpectedly or a client is nervous about the market. In times of uncertainty, perspective and trust matters.

AI can also track goal progress and recommend changes in saving habits or spending behaviors. It can recognize when a client is drifting off-course and help the advisor course-correct in real time.

In essence, AI becomes a partner in behavior coaching, one of the most valuable services a human advisor can offer. AI can do in days, what some advisors learn over years, but the advisor must verify the accuracy.

New Competitors and Business Models

AI is also lowering the barrier to entry for new firms. Fintech startups and big tech companies are offering sleek, AI-driven financial services with little overhead. They can scale quickly, attract younger clients, and operate at lower cost.

Some of these platforms use gamification, community features, and real-time insights to appeal to digital-native investors. Others provide low-cost subscriptions instead of traditional AUM-based pricing.

The "other" competitor now is clients that use AI to replace their current advisor. Some clients can ask frontier AI their financial questions directly, but where's the trust factor.

Client Adoption of AI

If AI is scraping the web to find answers, different AI tools will provide different answers for clients, depending on the inputs, and the tools used. How will a client know which one is accurate?

For clients to use AI to replace an advisor, the learning curve is greater than people really understand. Many people ask Chat GPT or Claude a financial question and get a quick answer. They then believe this can answer all their questions going forward. But it creates a new and unrealized issue for clients; they now must manage their finances on their own without accountability, and they need to learn what to ask.

But, for a client to be proficient in AI, they must have 3 things. They must have the time, the ability, and most of all, the willingness or desire to do it. Most people have one or two of these traits, but many do NOT have all three, which narrows down the number of clients willing to use AI, especially to replace financial planners.

Time: How many clients take the time to manage their finances efficiently now? Not many, which is why they need advisors and planners. While cool AI tools are fun to use for clients with a specific question, I don't believe clients will spend much more time digging into details than they have in the past, even with AI.

Ability: How many clients do we know that manage finances and investments efficiently? Sure, there are plenty of "do it yourselfers", but do they really know everything sufficiently or do they just think they know enough? In my 30 years' experience, the higher net-worth clients know enough to realize they need the help, even with AI. There are too many details to understand, and the more questions you ask AI, the more questions it creates, if done correctly.

Willingness: I also believe many clients simply don't want to deal with money issues. They'd rather spend time with family or hobbies having fun. And without the discipline to manage financial issues on a regular basis, AI won't help them. The accountability and follow up is why they need an advisor in the first place.

And as much as AI makes people feel smarter, people will not have the same knowledge as a professional advisor and won't know the right questions to ask the AI tool.

Furthermore, the AI tool will not provide them with much of a perspective. It'll only provide a black and white answer. Maybe this is enough for a simple question, but is it enough for a complex issue, especially if the client does not know the correct way to relate it to other financial questions? I think not, at least in the foreseeable future.

Clients can use AI to answer all their basic financial questions, but a financial plan is complex and has many components. Clients need someone they can trust to tell them things will be OK. They need someone they can trust to provide perspective on where they are in their financial journey. Regardless of how much financial data a client puts into AI, I doubt any AI tool will be able to replace the trust, perspective, and opinions provided by a financial advisor.

So, you can see this doesn't mean the traditional advisor is doomed. But it does mean they must evolve. The future belongs to advisors who offer deep expertise, human empathy, and holistic planning—not just investment picks.

The opportunity lies in offering a boutique, human-first experience that complements AI's speed and efficiency with personal relationships and long-term vision. But there will always be a subset of clients who don't want to manage their own portfolio or deal with their own financial issues, especially if they aren't tech savvy. These clients will always provide demand for financial advisors.

The Advisor Skill Shift

To succeed in an AI-enhanced future, advisors will need to develop new skills:

- Emotional intelligence and empathy: the ability to interpret client feelings and build trust, and implement these aspects into portfolios
- Estate, tax, and multi-generational planning: areas where AI offers support but not strategy
- Ethical awareness in data usage: ensuring privacy and consent in an AI-driven world

- Strategic thinking and scenario analysis: interpreting AI outputs in a broader financial context
- Trust and perspective from experience with similar situations and personal client awareness
- Learn how to direct AI by writing good instructions, reviewing output critically, and using the right tools (HumanAI has a tool called "Hope" which is built for that purpose.

Training programs and certifications will likely evolve to include AI literacy. Advisors who understand how to work with algorithms will gain an edge, much like those who once embraced Excel or financial planning software.

Soft skills, not spreadsheets, will become the advisor's greatest asset. Advisors who learn to interpret AI insights and translate them into meaningful conversations will have a lasting edge.

Not Everything on the Internet is True

AI gives us answers to questions instantaneously. We no longer must rely on our memory of tax brackets, IRA contribution limits, and taxable estate amounts. It does make our life easier. And it will do the same for clients, who may not need advisors as much as they used to.

But we must remember that AI is just what it says, Artificial Intelligence. There is a question of how much to trust it. I asked Google where AI gets its information from, and here's the response:

***AI models, especially generative ones, learn from vast amounts of data, including web scraping, public datasets, user-generated content, internal company data, and data licensed from third parties. Here's a more detailed breakdown of the sources:***

- ***Web Scraping and Crawling:***

  ***AI models can be trained by extracting data from websites, focusing on specific topics or information types.***

- ***Public Datasets:***

  ***Openly available datasets from institutions like governments and universities are used for AI training.***

- ***User-Generated Content (UGC):***

  ***Data from social media, reviews, and other user-generated content can be valuable for training.***

- ***Internal Company Data:***

  ***Organizations can use their own data, such as customer data, to train AI models for specific purposes.***

- ***Third-Party Data Vendors:***

  ***Companies specialize in collecting and selling data, which can be used by AI developers.***

- ***Synthetic Data Generation:***

  ***AI can be used to create synthetic data, which can then be used to train other AI models, especially when real-world data is limited or sensitive.***

- ***Crowdsourcing:***

  ***Companies can use online platforms to hire and manage crowds to gather data.***

- ***APIs (Application Programming Interfaces):***

  ***Many AI systems interact with external services and databases through APIs.***

- ***Databases and Knowledge Bases:***

  ***AI systems can be integrated with databases and knowledge bases containing vast amounts of information.***

Generative AI is experimental.

Thank you, Google! This is interesting to see that some of the things we do with AI, are repurposed to in the web scraping for more AI. So, the more information society contributes to AI, the more society gets out of it. But how do we know if it's accurate?

I asked an editor at a major news publication about this. She told me a story of a researcher who used AI to pull together a list of authors for a research project. AI generated a list of bibliographies for information for the project. When the researcher tried to look up the publications, they didn't exist. Then the editor I called suggested that I Google "AI Hallucinations". Here again is how Google replied:

***AI hallucinations refer to instances where artificial intelligence (AI) models generate incorrect, misleading, or fabricated information. These hallucinations can occur when AI models:***

- ***Make inaccurate assumptions:***

  ***AI models may base their inferences on incomplete or biased data, leading to errors in judgment.***

- ***Overfit to training data:***

  ***If an AI model is trained on a limited dataset, it may become overly sensitive to the patterns within that data, generating outputs that are not generalizable to real-world situations.***

- ***Lack common sense:***

  ***AI models often lack the ability to understand real-world context and logic, which can result in nonsensical or contradictory outputs.***

- ***Encounter ambiguity:***

  ***Natural language is inherently ambiguous, and AI models may struggle to interpret ambiguous prompts or data, leading to hallucinations.***

***AI hallucinations can range from minor factual errors to serious safety issues, especially in applications where AI is used for decision-making or information generation. It's important to be aware of the potential for AI hallucinations and to critically evaluate the outputs generated by AI models.***

Generative AI is experimental.

Notice at the end of each Google response, even Google says, "Generative AI is experimental". All of this doesn't mean that AI is incorrect, but it does mean to trust but verify. If machine learning is giving us information from which to make decisions, we need to be careful to not rely solely on this information all the time, without meticulous verification.

Final Thoughts: Embrace the Opportunity but Keep it in Perspective

And just in case you were wondering, yes, I asked AI to help generate much of the content for this chapter, and I reviewed and modified it for accuracy. But don't worry, none of the other chapters were written by AI!

AI will not replace financial advisors. But it will replace the parts of their job that can be automated, optimized, or digitized. Advisors who cling to outdated methods risk being left behind, while advisors who embrace technology and AI will find their profession more comprehensive, streamlined, and more rewarding.

But those advisors who embrace AI as a partner, not a threat, will find themselves empowered like never before. With the right mindset and tools, the advisor of the future will be more efficient, more insightful, and more indispensable than ever.

The real question is not whether AI will change wealth management. It already has. The question is: how and when you will adapt, not if you will adapt. Now let's talk about the rules for using AI in the next chapter.

## CHAPTER 10

# Using AI Without Losing Your License

What does this mean? It means compliance, compliance, and then some more compliance. I know you don't want to read about compliance, but stay with me here. I say it this way because independent advisors find compliance to be one of their biggest struggles. They don't have a hard time staying compliant, they have a hard time managing the compliance tasks and incorporating them into their daily routine. Let's face it, no one wakes up every day and gets excited about doing compliance chores!

When I started my practice, I tried to streamline my compliance chores so much that I started a software company to do this! Don't ever do that, and I won't ever do that again. While I'm no longer involved in the company, we still use it, and the company continues to evolve in ways to address current regulations, which means I don't have to be a compliance expert.

Some people think compliance only matters when you get audited. I completely disagree. The priority in compliance is the fiduciary standard, which applies to everything we do, every day. And if you don't know what that is, you probably don't need to be an advisor.

The fiduciary standard doesn't have an AI counterpart. This standard relies solely on the morals, ethics, and integrity of the advisor. AI cannot replace that ability but might be able to identify a mistake after it's too late. The point is, every advisor is responsible for advice, communications, decision making, and data handling regardless of what tool produced the recommendation. And an examiner will not accept the excuse of, "AI did it". But here are a few examples of AI topics that must be addressed in your compliance procedures.

AI washing. I believe compliance will continue to get more complex and require more time to manage it correctly. Yes, AI can help manage tasks, but as stated before, the advisor is where the buck stops. The SEC's first AI enforcement was for firms overstating their use of AI in marketing and in compliance documents such as ADV's, also known as AI washing. If you use AI to generate these documents, do NOT overstate or understate any issues. Different AI agents have varying outputs and can demonstrate different perspectives. And some advisors believe the longer documents are more appealing to examiners. This is not the case, if the content is exaggerated or is just fluff. These documents should be clear, concise, and accurate, nothing else.

The Marketing Rule vs AI content. AI lets you produce 100x the content we once used with exceptional creativity and depth. But the bottleneck here is that every piece of marketing material still needs compliance review. It's so easy to just, "skip reviewing this one" because it's like the last one and, "not much has changed". But the minute this habit begins, the sooner you will be in trouble.

AI-generated ads, social posts, and lead-generation sequences are still advertisements under Rule 206(4)-1: substantiation, no misleading performance claims or testimonial rules. And volume IS the trap here. But it's all fine if you manage it well, review it for compliance, and create a compliance archive for everything.

Client data and privacy. This is important and frequently overlooked. I'm going to combine this concept with something called vendor due diligence. The urgency here is understand that any confidential client information input into AI, is a violation of Personally Identifiable Information (PII). AI actually diasagreed with me on this! But as most AI software's use data from the internet to provide solutions, they'll also put your data back out there for others to use. And if you use PII in your inputs for AI, it's a clear violation of the privacy rules.

Any violation of these regulations means you must go through a protocol to identify the information that was compromised, and you are responsible for the potential damages. Reg S-P safeguards and incident response and client notification requirements are becoming the norm, and they can vary by state.

This also means you must demand more information from your vendors. If you use a financial planning software that uses PII, you better ask them how their data is secured, where it is stored, who has access to it, and what happens if there is a breach.

This includes internal books and records. AI generated client communications, meeting summaries, and chat logs are all records that must now be stored securely with the same parameters as your vendors. (Rule 204-2) The off-channel-communications enforcement is a new standard. You must store this information, including text messages and email, and you must store it securely.

Do you have a written AI policy? If you don't already, you need one. There are requirements for listing approved vendors, prohibited uses for AI, AI review requirements, disclosure language, and training. And according to compliance-program rule (206(4)-7), even your annual review with clients should now cover the use of AI.

Regulatory Weather. Yes, the regulations must be somewhat predictive. What does that mean? It means the examination storms tend to move around different topics, many related to AI. While some regulations already cover AI, you should document your reasoning because the examinations routinely ask about AI. FINRA and NASAA are actively doing this. But if you stay ahead of it, these procedures are only adjustments rather than emergencies.

Cybersecurity. We must spend a few minutes talking about this. The criminals are using AI much faster than advisors and clients. The cybersecurity risks are growing stronger every day, and the processes to address these risks are getting more complex and expensive. But you cannot overlook these things because they will eventually apply to you.

Here is a quick, real-life example of an advisor friend of mine, who has been independent for many years, but operated under a local RIA. He had a sophisticated client for a few years who invested $1.4 million, mostly in IRA funds. One day the client asked for a large withdrawal to invest in a cryptocurrency account somewhere else. The advisor reluctantly agreed to transfer the funds but advised the client he would owe tax on the distribution. Over the course of the next few months, the client stated he was doubling his money and continued to withdraw funds until he had withdrawn ALL his investments from the publicly traded accounts, and over half of these funds were IRA funds.

The advisor continued to explain this was a bad idea, but the client wouldn't listed because he was making so much money. Then the client asked for a withdrawal to pay the taxed owed on the distributions. His entire crypto account disappeared, and the money was gone…all of it. Not only did he lose $1.4 million, but he also owed over $400,000 in tax to the IRS and had no more funds to pay it.

The reason I bring this up is because the client then found an attorney who sued the advisor for a "breach of fiduciary duty by allowing the client to withdraw the funds". The advisor did everything correctly and was still sued for the entire amount. You can't make this stuff up!

It was OK in the end because the RIA the advisor was using had good E&O insurance, and the claim is still being defended by the insurance company. But, had the advisor been completely independent, this might have put him out of business, regardless of who is right or wrong. The cybersecurity issues are real problems that advisors need to be prepared to address. And the Fiduciary Rule was the essential "Golden Rule" here. As we discussed previously, if you use the fiduciary standard in all applications, and apply some basic business practices, most risks will be covered.

<u>Compliance Summary</u>. These are only a few specific compliance issues, primarily relating to AI. I can't even begin to provide a compliance outline for you. You must use a professional consultant or attorney for this. But, compliance in general is one of the most

time-consuming challenges of running an independent practice. If you can't use technology to offset the tasks, the compliance alone can become overwhelming. Don't overthink it but use the tools available at your discretion. Or work with an RIA firm who will allow you to own your own book of business but will also handle the compliance organization for you.

I've heard many advisors make the statement, "Joining an RIA is too expensive, even if I still own my own book". But it's a simple math issue. If the RIA you are joining takes 25-30% of your revenue but saves you 40% of your time so you can build a practice, the math works. And if you aren't spending 40% of your time working through the infrastructure and compliance planning, you are already in trouble. You must use a compliance software, you must have E&O insurance, and you must have a compliance consultant or attorney. And the costs for these services are similar if you manage $5 million or $50 million, so you must factor this into your business plan and your expenses.

Whichever path you chose, do it deliberately and control the process. Therefore, it will not control you and you won't have to stay awake at night worrying about an exam.

# CHAPTER 11

# The Relationship Aspect

This is a tough one. There are many ways to manage relationships with clients. And typically, the relationship aspect varies from client to client. Some clients want to be friends. Some clients don't want to be friends. Some clients want to know enough personal information about us to understand our philosophies and processes, without getting too close. And some clients want to come to our office to validate that we are a real business. But regardless of the level of personal interaction, and I can't stress this enough, clients want to trust us enough to know that we can handle the responsibility they've given us.

And it's a lot of responsibility. But it's also about perspective. We deal with financial issues for clients every day. We have the licensing and training to help them make decisions that will affect them for the rest of their lives. And clients need to be able to talk to us about things they can't ask anyone else. It's common for some clients to ask us financial questions they don't ask their spouse about, not because they don't trust their spouse, but because their spouse may not be financially engaged.

Now we've come full circle to the type of practice we want to build. I'll acknowledge that we must take all clients when we start in the business because we must pay the bills. But over time, advisors should focus on a specific subset of clients, where the advisor feels comfortable giving advice. Therefore, it's helpful for us as advisors to limit the demographics of our client base to have similarities in financial stages for clients, similar ideologies, and similar financial philosophies.

You can manage clients with broad range of financial levels, but it's not efficient, and you may not give the best advice if you are relating your experience with a high-net-worth client to someone who is a new investor, and vice versa.

Remember that clients need to trust us. The best way to accomplish this is by eliminating anything that might make a client or prospect wonder "why" they should use your services. This includes how we dress, how we let them talk, and what our office environment looks like. These details matter. And it only takes one small thing to make a client question your decision-making ability.

But once the trust is established, clients need to share all their financial concerns, issues, and sometimes grief. Clearly, advisors 'discussions with clients sometimes become more therapeutic in nature than financial. And this is a great step in relationship building, but don't forget why they are there. Advisors must stay the course and accomplish the financial goals during meetings, even if most of the meeting is consumed with personal issues or family problems that don't relate to the financial strategy.

A few other comments about meetings with clients or prospects is to never, ever talk about politics or religion. Remember your place as their financial advisor, not their preacher, and not their politician. This again can cause more damage than harm if they think you are more concerned about politics than you are concerned about managing their financial affairs. We must always remain confident, professional, and true to the financial discussions.

But we must also make the meetings enjoyable, and even fun. Remember that clients and prospects don't want to meet with us, just like they don't want to meet with their CPA. The more we can create an environment of enjoyment, the more they'll open up and the more they'll want to come back and visit again. Tell stories to help them relate to you. And it's OK to show vulnerability. Clients need to know we are being honest, and sometimes, the best way to demonstrate that is talking about mistakes, not just talking about how good we are at our job.

Then there are the clients that simply hire us to do a job. There's nothing wrong with it. I once met with a married couple and was working really hard to gain their trust and make friends with them. About halfway through the meeting, she interrupted me and said, "let me be clear, we don't need to be friends with you, we're paying you to do a job, and that's why we are here". She set the parameters of the relationship that has lasted over 15 years. But we always know where we stand and what we need to discuss each year when we meet with them. And frankly, I've always appreciated her honesty.

Regarding client relationships, I want to talk about one more aspect, which is handling financial affairs for friends and family. It's common to become friends with clients, and it's common to have friends and family to ask us to become clients. That's how our business works. But be careful to set the parameters of the working relationship up front. For example, I've told my friends and family they need to ask me about their financial affairs during business hours and not discuss this at family gatherings such as Thanksgiving dinner. First, it's unprofessional to talk about specifics when we, as the advisor, don't have information in front of us. And it's also difficult to keep information confidential in this type of setting. But more importantly, discussing financial affairs in a personal or family environment can change a personal relationship into a business relationship, which can forever change the context of your discussions. And you don't want to talk business every time to see your friends and family.

I've been forced to revisit this with one family member multiple times. While he's a dear friend, I've had to fire him as a client twice. He was just not able to separate the business from pleasure, and all our social visits became work meetings. I finally referred him to an advisor in our office, which allowed me to tell him, "I don't know, call your advisor", every time he asked these questions in a family setting. This worked out well.

As you can see, managing relationships is a difficult aspect of our job as financial advisors. We must spend more time listening than talking, but we must talk enough to make clients feel comfortable. It's common for young advisors to spend time talking about what they can do to help, when it's too early in the relationship, and the client feels interrupted. This is a huge mistake. If we can learn to manage the relationship aspect, which is different for each client, the trust will happen quicker. At the end of each meeting, every client just wants to know they'll be OK, and they want to hear it from an advisor whose perspective they trust and respect.

# CHAPTER 12

# How Much is it Worth?

At the end of an advisor's career, their business should be more than just a list of clients—it should be a valuable asset. Whether you plan to sell your practice, transition it to a successor, or simply wind it down, succession planning and business valuation should be part of your long-term strategy.

This chapter explores how to structure your practice for maximum value, understand industry multiples, and determine who you'd sell it to.

Lifestyle Practice vs. Scalable Business—What's Your Goal?

Every advisor's career fall into one of two categories (they are both great):

1. The Lifestyle Practice

A lifestyle practice is built around personal income and flexibility rather than growth.
✓ You maximize earnings during your career but may not build an easily sellable business.
✓ Clients work with you personally, making transition difficult.
✓ You may not have formalized processes or systems in place for succession.

💡 Best suited for advisors who want to work until retirement but don't necessarily plan to sell their book of business. Perhaps they wind it down during retirement but continue to work late into life. But this is a much more personable approach, and the relationships are much deeper.

2. The Scalable Business

A scalable business is built with long-term value in mind.
✓ Client relationships are based on the firm, not just you.
✓ Processes, tech, and teams are structured for growth.
✓ It's easier to sell, merge, or transition because it operates independently of any one advisor.

💡 Best suited for advisors who want to build a practice with exit value and long-term sustainability. This type of practice is much easier to sell because the clients are not as reliant on the relationship as they are on the "commoditized service" provided.

🚀 Which one are you building? If you plan to sell, your goal should be a scalable business. If you plan to work with your families for decades, you should focus on personal relationships with all your clients.

Perhaps the best path is a combination of the two. But it's also the hardest path, especially if you wait to adopt technology, processes, and scalability.

What Are Industry Multiples for RIAs & BD Books of Business?

If you plan to sell, you need to understand valuation.

◇ RIA (Registered Investment Advisor) Firms – Typically valued at 2.5x to 4x revenue.
◇ BD (Broker-Dealer) Books of Business – Generally valued at 0.8x to 2.5x revenue.

Why the difference?

- RIAs generate recurring revenue (AUM fees), making them more valuable.

- BD books rely more on commissions, which are harder to sustain long-term.

💰 Factors That Affect Valuation:
✓ Recurring revenue vs. transactional revenue – The more predictable your income, the better.
✓ Client demographics – A book full of young clients = higher value. An aging client base = lower value.
✓ Firm structure – If your practice can run without you, it's worth more.
✓ Growth rate – Buyers pay a premium for books that are still growing.
📈 The 10% Rule: Small Growth, Big Impact

Every percentage point of growth directly impacts valuation. If your book of business grows by just 10% more per year organically, the long-term impact on valuation is substantial.

Organic growth. This is the growth that really matters. Your practice should grow from your existing clients without ANY effort. It's the best gauge of the job you are doing and the value your clients are getting from you. If there's no growth, you should evaluate your value proposition to your clients, put out the surveys and respond to their feedback. It's never too late to change how you operate your practice. This clearly relies on a strong service model.

Inorganic growth. This is growth that is generated purely by growth activities such as buying leads or buying a practice. Obviously, this is the primary engine that builds a practice, especially in the early years when there aren't enough clients in the practice to rely on referrals. This clearly relies on a strong sales model.

Market growth. This is a given factor, sort of. Many advisors rely on this growth every year, and it's a real bonus, until it isn't. I think it's a mistake to factor this into your growth proforma. If you've been through a "real" market downturn, you've seen how this works out, and it's devastating to advisors who plan on this growth for the revenue projections and practice valuations. These economic downturns are when you'll see these advisors sell their practice. If the growth happens every year, that's great. Add the increased revenue to your practice valuation, but don't count on it for the following year until it happens.

Who Would You Sell It To?

If you're thinking about selling, consider who your buyer might be.

1. Internal Succession (Junior Advisor)

✓ Train and transition your business to a younger advisor in your firm.
✓ Often structured as a buyout over time.
✓ Keeps client relationships intact.

2. External Buyer (Another RIA or BD Firm)

✓ Sell to a larger firm that wants to acquire your book.
✓ Typically offers a higher multiple but may require changes in how clients are serviced.

3. Private Equity / Aggregators

✓ Large PE firms are buying up advisory practices.
✓ These deals often offer higher upfront cash but may include earn-out periods.

4. Selling to a Competitor

✓ If you have a strong local brand, a nearby competitor may want to acquire your book.
✓ Usually structured as a gradual transition to avoid client disruption.

⬣ Key Question: How Will Clients React?
No matter who you sell to, client retention is critical. Buyers will assess how likely your clients are to stay after the transition.

Statistics vs. Specifics – What's the Difference?

Many advisors focus on broad industry statistics, but what really matters is your specific numbers.

📊 Industry Stat – "The average RIA sells for 2.5x revenue."
📈 Your Specifics – If your client base is growing, diversified, and has strong recurring revenue, your multiple could be higher.

◇ Know Your Data:
✓ Revenue breakdown (AUM fees vs. commissions)
✓ Client age demographics
✓ Retention rate and referral growth
✓ Operational efficiency (tech, team, processes)

💡 Buyers don't just buy revenue—they buy certainty and sustainability. And the values are determined by the statistics of a practice. When a buyer asks a seller the average age of a client, too many advisors will say "about 65". That's a clear indication the advisor does NOT know this number, or any other major statistic about their practice.

To go further into this discussion, these vague responses also mean the advisor is running a lifestyle practice more than a scalable practice that has embraced technology to analyze the numbers. But if or when an advisor begins thinking about selling a practice, these demographics and financial statistics are crucial, and they'll ultimately add a lot of value to the practice valuation.

But there's one more important thing to remember. Let's come back to the theory of business owners' relying on the value of their business as their personal retirement plan. As I've said a few times already, as financial planners, we need to take our own advice. We would always tell clients to have retirement plans, have buy-sell agreements and insurance policies, etc. We should do this for ourselves and our practices as well. Advisors should always remember to take their own advice.

Final Thought: Build for the Future, Not Just Today

- If you want to maximize your exit, start planning now.
- Shift from a lifestyle practice to a scalable business model.
- Focus on recurring revenue and structured processes.
- Identify potential buyers before you're ready to sell.

A financial advisory business isn't just about today's income—it's a long-term asset. Build it with the end in mind.

## CHAPTER 13

# Can You Do It? Maybe...

Not every financial advisor is cut out for entrepreneurship. And like we've discussed; financial advisors do NOT make good businesspeople. While the idea of running your own practice sounds appealing—freedom, unlimited earning potential, and control over your destiny—it comes with significant challenges. Before you take the leap, it's crucial to conduct an honest self-assessment. And frankly, many of these concepts will apply if you are independent or if you work for a larger firm.

This chapter will help you evaluate your suitability for entrepreneurship and explore alternative paths, such as partnerships or hybrid models, for those who may not want to go fully independent.

It's Not as Easy as You Think

Owning your own practice means being responsible for every aspect of the business. There is no safety net—no guaranteed paycheck, no employer-sponsored benefits, and no built-in client base. Instead, success depends entirely on your ability to generate business, manage operations, and stay disciplined every day.

Here are some of the key requirements for financial advisors considering entrepreneurship:

1. Risk Taking

Starting your own practice means stepping into uncertainty. There will be months—possibly years—where you may not see consistent income. You must be comfortable making decisions with incomplete information, investing in your business with no guaranteed return, and dealing with the possibility of failure. If you prefer security over opportunity, entrepreneurship may not be the best path for you.

2. Hard Work Every Day-You Must Do the Work

Entrepreneurial advisors don't work 9-to-5; they work until the job is done. Whether it's prospecting new clients, handling compliance requirements, or managing administrative tasks, there's always something to do. Success isn't about working long hours—it's about using those hours effectively and working until the task are completed, regardless of how long it takes.

3. Discipline to Focus

Distractions are everywhere, especially when you don't have a boss or corporate structure holding you accountable. Entrepreneurs need the discipline to structure their day, prioritize high-impact activities, and resist the urge to procrastinate. If you struggle with time management, independence might be overwhelming. And if you aren't organized enough to have a solid plan, your unallocated time will turn into unproductive time, when it should be your most productive time.

It's easy to get distracted looking at investments or finding the next best software that creates cool graphs for clients. In reality, you'll need to initially focus on business development rather than the fun stuff like tech toys. These distractions will cause you to wake up a year or two later and wonder why you aren't making enough money to pay your bills. At that point, your options will be more limited.

4. Financial Sacrifice

Starting a business requires financial investment and patience. You may have to forgo a steady paycheck, dip into savings, or reinvest earnings into your practice. Many successful advisors go years without making what they would have in a salaried position—but long-term rewards often justify the initial sacrifice.

On a personal note, my wife and I sacrificed over 10 years of retirement savings to start our practice. But we had the business experience, the industry knowledge, and the social network to make it work. More importantly, we had the confidence and willingness to take the risk and know it would work.

5. Industry Knowledge

You can't advise clients on wealth-building if you don't understand the markets, tax laws, investment strategies, and financial planning principles. But beyond technical knowledge, you must also understand the business side of financial advising—marketing, compliance, client acquisition, and retention strategies. We've discussed this previously, but I cannot adequately emphasize the responsibility that comes with sitting down in front of a client and making recommendations, and them implementing them later. These decisions can be life altering for your clients. Advisors must know their limits and when to ask for help. If you do NOT know who to ask for help, you should join a firm who can provide those resources. It's much cheaper to buy the tech tools and resources than it is to reinvent the wheel and build it yourself.

What Makes a Good Advisor?

Regardless of whether you work for a firm or start your own practice, there are certain traits that separate great advisors from average ones:

1. Knowledgeable

Clients trust advisors with their financial futures, so you need deep expertise. Continuing education, staying current with industry trends, and knowing how to explain complex financial concepts in simple terms are essential.

2. Good at Sales-by your own definition

Even if you don't consider yourself a "salesperson," financial advising is fundamentally a sales role. You must be able to present solutions, gain trust, and convince people to act in their best interest. If you struggle with sales, you may need to develop this skill before considering entrepreneurship.

3. Strong Organizational Skills

Balancing multiple clients, tracking investments, handling paperwork, and keeping up with regulations all require a high level of organization. Without proper systems, things can quickly fall apart.

4. Ability to Relate to People & Be Empathetic

Beyond numbers, this business is about people. Clients want an advisor who understands their goals, fears, and emotions. The ability to connect, listen, and provide guidance tailored to each client is what builds long-term relationships and referrals.

Finally, and most importantly, you need a plan. Do not take the chance and hope it works. As we all know, hope is not a strategy. Your plan should address all the components of your vision for your practice. More about this in the next chapter.

Is This a Job or a Career? The difference between a job and a career is commitment.

If you see financial advising as just a way to earn a paycheck, where you quit work at 5:00 every day and don't think about it until the next morning, you may not have the mindset to run your own practice. Entrepreneurship requires constant learning, improvement, and problem-solving—even outside of business hours.

But if you find yourself thinking about how to improve your service, build better relationships, grow your own business, or solve a client's challenge outside of working hours, then financial advising might not just be a job—it could be your passion and career.

Not everyone is meant to be an entrepreneur, and that's okay. Some advisors thrive in a structured firm environment, while others prefer the freedom of independence. The key is knowing yourself—your strengths, weaknesses, and what truly motivates you. So, can you do it? Maybe, but only if you're willing to embrace the risks, put in the work, and commit to continuous growth, regardless of the challenges and setbacks.

CHAPTER 14

# Here's what I think

There's a lot to consider when thinking about becoming and advisor or owning your own practice. And the personality types required for this profession are typically folks who are motivated, impatient, over achievers. Because these personalities typically lack patience, this can lead to making mistakes. Let's talk about some of these aspects.

Mistakes are going to happen. Do what you can to prevent them, but when they happen, own them. We talked about this previously, but this is sometimes the best way to learn the industry, learn our own limits, and learn how to do things differently. If we learn from each mistake, share it with others to help them learn, and we don't EVER make the same mistake again, it will translate into invaluable experience.

But we also must have the right attitude. We cannot just push through the process of building a practice without any thought to the details and consequences of our actions, both for ourselves, for our clients, and for our coworkers. Success comes at a price. And we make a conscious decision to pay that price whether it's in dollars that we've set aside for the growth of our business of if the price is time that don't have for our friends and family or hobbies. My point is that every advisor should evaluate how much of a sacrifice they are willing to pay and be careful to not overpay it. It's too easy to get wrapped up in work and "spend time with the kids later". This never works and you'll lose time and experiences you can never get back.

I would also argue the other side of this by saying there is a price to be paid for doing nothing. I believe too many advisors are stuck in a position they don't like because the fear of change has continually prevented them from stepping out to build their own practice. This has a different cost associated with it. The cost is frustration, income limitations, and a personal growth ceiling. Building a practice and spending time with family, friends or other priorities, are not mutually exclusive. But it requires a process of consciously planning out the business plan, the time allocation, and sacrifices to implement the plan.

This profession is hard. It's difficult to get started. It's tough to grow, and then it's tough to manage. These are choices that must be made. We are better to make them on our own, instead of having these choices made for us. Our habits, our personal rules, and our work ethic will help us stay the course. Remember that integrity is what we do when no one is looking. These strengths will prove invaluable as we embark down the path of building our own practice. And you must do the work!

But also remember this is a team sport. There's no need to reinvent the wheel and recreate things that have already been done. Not utilizing the tools, experience, and mentorship that's available means you'll be paying a higher price (dollars, time, or both), than necessary. But with the right attitude and conviction to doing the right thing, you can minimize those "costs".

In my experience, I've made many mistakes which have affected advisors' success rates by allowing them to become advisors or own their own practice when they were clearly NOT ready to do so. Either they didn't have the business acumen, the client relational skills, or the monetary staying power, or the discipline to stay in it until they were successful. The end result was advisors who had to take other jobs to pay their bills, or advisors who lost clients because they didn't know how to build relationships even after they gained the accounts. It's hard to watch advisors make the same mistakes I've made, which is why I chose to outline the concepts here.

The details matter, so if you've skimmed through these topics and not caught the details that are buried in the content, you've likely missed some of the best nuggets. This is true with building a practice as well.

If you skipped over a detail because you didn't have time, you'll have to address it eventually. You might as well pay attention early, even though you'll work harder than you ever have in the early years. But it will be worth it in the long run, and you'll be better at your profession. I would suggest reading a book called "Deep Work", by Cal Newport. While it doesn't relate to our profession, it discusses how to be the best at whatever you've chosen to do in life.

But beyond that, being an advisor is tougher than it looks from outside of our profession. We must be all things to everybody, and clients don't care about our problems. They need our confirmation that everything will be OK. This means we must be good at sales, we must know how to service accounts, we must know how to relate to clients individually, and we must adopt technology to manage our practice. Very few people are good at mastering all these skills simultaneously.

But again, when we sit down in front of a client, none of these things matter if we don't know how to relate to them, help with their problem, and build a relationship. At the end of the day, clients want to know they'll be OK. And if they aren't going to be OK, what do they need to do to be OK. We must determine the best environment to be able to do this for them, and there are many options.

In our industry, 40% of financial advisors will retire in the next 10 years. There is a huge opportunity for new advisors with the right perspective and the willingness to adapt and learn. Yes, AI will change the industry somewhat, but it will also create opportunities we don't yet understand. If you think about how things will look in 10 years with AI helping the 60% of advisors left in the business, with potentially the same number of clients, you can begin to grasp the opportunities.

Therefore, with time, experience, mentorship, and a few mistakes, it's the best profession for folks willing to work hard, evolve their skillsets, and grow with their clients. But if you think it's easy, or if you think anyone can do it, you'll need to read this again☺.

# Appendix

## Spreadsheets

### Annual planning spreadsheet

| **Adviosr Name** | **Jane example** |
|---|---|
| Current Year | |
| Current # of clients | 50 |
| Average AUM per client HH | $250,000 |
| Total current AUM | $12,500,000 |
| Average Fee % | 1.10% |
| Total current gross production | $137,500.00 |
| | |
| **Assumptions for next year** | |
| Additional production goal in dollars | $250,000 |
| Assumed average AUM for new client | $350,000 |
| Assumed fee % for new accounts | 1.25% |
| Number of clients needed (12 months) | 57.14 |
| Clients needed per month | 4.76 |
| | |
| Average assumed closing ratio | 50.00% |
| Prospect meetings needed per month to meet goal | 9.52 |
| | |
| **Activities to attain desired meetings per month** | |
| COI meetings | 9.52 |
| Marketing research meetings/calls | 2 |
| Business development meetings-networking | 4 |
| Current client reviews per month (ask for referrals) | 4.17 |
| | |
| Total meetings per month for goal | 19.69 |
| | |
| Call or emails required to get meetings (assumed 4x) | 78.76 |

Denotes manual data input fields

# Practice Proforma

| Year end | | 2025 | 2026 | 2027 |
|---|---|---|---|---|
| Existing advisor growth | 25% | | | |
| Additional AUM (per planning meeting) | | $77 | $94 | $118 |
| Current AUM (millions) | $300 | $377 | $471 | $589 |
| New advisors per year | $2 | $2 | $2 | $2 |
| AUM per new advisor ($millions) | $10 | $20 | $20 | $20 |
| Growth per new advisor | 25% | | $5 | $10 |
| Total AUM on current path (millions) | | $397 | $496 | $619 |
| Total Revenue (millions) | 1% | $4 | $5 | $6 |
| Company Revenue (millions) | 25% | $1 | $1 | $2 |

# Marketing Summary

| **Sample marketing comparisons**<br>Updated 2025 | **Company 1** | **Company 2** | **Company 3** | **Company 4** | **Company 5** | **Company 6** | **Company 7** | **Company 8** | **Company 9** |
|---|---|---|---|---|---|---|---|---|---|
| | Linked In<br>Sales Navigator<br>Proprietary<br>Proprietary | Direct marketing<br>Forbes<br>Bloomberg | Direct mkting | Direct Marketing | Appt setting only<br>Text<br>Emails<br>Event driven | Email marketing<br>Newspaper<br>Online | Social media only<br>Linked In<br>FB<br>Instagram | Marketing firm | Social Media<br>Instagram<br>Email<br>Text |
| Term period | 12 months | 4 months | Monthly | Annually | 3 months | 6 mpnths | | | Annual |
| Set up Fee | $5,000 | $15,000 | | $3,000 | $20,000 | $0 | $1,000 | 5000 | |
| Monthly fee or ad spend | $500 | $4,500 | $1,500 | $1,000 | $1,000 | $3,000 | $1,000 | 4000 | 3000 |
| Leads per month | Maybe | 10 | 20 | 5 | No-must provide | 12 emails to website | | | |
| Appointments per month | No | 10 (Virtual only) | No | No | 40-60 | 3 | | | |
| Average AUM per lead | Unknown | $500k | 450k | 250k-500k | 500k | 1000000 | | | |
| Content provided | No | yes | N/A | N/A | No-must provide | Built with me | | | |
| Activities Required | Check messages daily<br>Respond with meeting requests<br>Convert to appointmens | Daily messaging | On demand calls | On demand calls | Content push | reply to emails<br>Set up appts | | | |
| Best to recruit (Clients or Advisors) | Advisors | Clients | Clients | Clients | Clients | Clients | Both | Clients | Clients |
| Technology required | Linked in<br>Calendly<br>FMG<br>Hubspot/Wealthbox | Proprietary<br>Calendly<br>FMG<br>Hubspot/Wealthbox | Proprietary CRM<br>Calendly<br>FMG<br>Hubspot/Wealthbox | Calendly<br>FMG<br>Hubspot/Wealthbox | Calendly<br>FMG<br>Hubspot/Wealthbox | New landing page<br>Calendly<br>FMG<br>Hubspot/Wealthbox | Calendly<br>FMG<br>Hubspot/Wealthbox | Calendly<br>FMG<br>Hubspot/Wealthbox | Calendly<br>FMG<br>Hubspot/Wealthbox |
| Additional seats for advisors | No | Yes for $5k setup fee | No | No | | | | | |
| Comments | Includes weekly call for 6 weeks<br>to build Linked In profile and | They set apptmnts<br>They build profile<br>They create messages | Needs absolute attention<br>Low close ration 5-10% | Needs absolute attention<br>Low close ration 5-10% | Buy leads from list svcs<br>does all automation<br>High volume<br>Prefer group meetings | 6640 targets<br>$700 Contextual<br>$1475-emails<br>$750 retargeting | Must build platform<br>Uses only social media<br>Use current "friends" | Build Websites<br>Build custom content<br>SEO work | Conversational Mkting |
| Contacts | | | | | | | | | |
| Leads per month | 20.00 | 10.00 | 20.00 | 20.00 | 40.00 | 3.00 | 10.00 | | |
| Avg AUM per Leads | 250,000.00 | $1,000,000 | $500,000 | $375,000 | $500,000 | $1,000,000 | $250,000 | | |
| Close ratio | 25% | 20% | 10% | 10% | 10% | 25% | 25% | | |
| Avg AUM closed per month | 1,250,000.00 | 2,000,000.00 | 1,000,000.00 | 750,000.00 | 2,000,000.00 | 750,000.00 | 625,000.00 | 0.00 | 0.00 |
| Annual AUM expected | 15,000,000.00 | 24,000,000.00 | 12,000,000.00 | 9,000,000.00 | 24,000,000.00 | 9,000,000.00 | 7,500,000.00 | 0.00 | 0.00 |
| Cost per year (12 mos avg w setup) | $11,000 | $69,000 | $18,000 | $15,000 | $32,000 | $36,000 | $13,000 | $53,000 | $36,000 |
| Cost per $1mm AUM | $733.33 | $2,875.00 | $1,500.00 | $1,666.67 | $1,333.33 | $4,000.00 | $1,733.33 | #DIV/0! | #DIV/0! |
| ROI @ 1% | | | | | | | | | |
| Pros | Good marketing and education on<br>building sequences to be handled<br>every month going forward | They handle everything<br>Use AI | | | | Local marketing | Mac | | |
| Cons | No direct lead gen | Expensive<br>Nationwide<br>All virtual | | | | Need content<br>Need landing page | Need content<br>Need landing page<br>Need sequencing<br># of leads expected?<br>Ad spend? | | |

www.ingramcontent.com/pod-product-compliance
Lightning Source LLC
LaVergne TN
LVHW051932051126
851857LV00020B/2076
* 9 7 9 8 9 5 2 0 3 0 4 1 1 *